D-Day Hero Destroyer Identified After 68 Year Search

by

Ray Woods

RoseDog Books

PITTSBURGH, PENNSYLVANIA 15222

RoseDog Books
701 Smithfield Street
Pittsburgh, PA 15222
Visit our website at *www.rosedogbookstore.com*

ISBN: 978-1-4349-3477-2
eISBN: 978-1-4349-3355-3

D-Day Hero Destroyer Identified
After 68 Year Search

Geri
Hope you enjoy this true history of WW II
Ray Woods

World War II Honoree

World War II Veteran

Raymond P. Woods

BRANCH OF
SERVICE
U.S. Navy

HOMETOWN
Ottawa, OH

ACTIVITY DURING WWII
SERVED AS A RADARMAN ON THE USS O'BRIEN DD-725. SERVED
AT D-DAY OMAHA BEACH AND THE BOMBARDMENT OF
CHERBOURG. CARRIER RAIDS ON LUZON AND JAPAN.
PARTICIPATED IN INVASIONS OF ORMOC BAY. MINDORO.
LUZON IN THE PHILIPPINES. IWO JIMA. KERAMA RETTO AND
OKINAWA.

Author: Raymond P. Woods

TABLE OF CONTENTS

In a 1995 article in the Spring Issue of
"Destroyers at War" called "Born to Fight"
A.B. Feuer wrote about the USS O'Brien DD725,

"Within a few short months of being commissioned,
the big, new 2200-ton Sumner-class destroyer O'Brien
found itself slugging it out with German shore batteries
during the tumultuous D-Day invasion of Normandy.
weaned in battle and led by a veteran skipper,
she gave as well as she took from the Germans –
then steamed into equally vicious battle against the Japanese
and the dreaded kamikazes of the Pacific War
to win six battle stars in an amazingly short time."

BY A. B. FEUER

CHAPTER 1

My name is Raymond (Ray) Woods and this is the story of my two years aboard the USS O'Brien DD725.

On a beautiful August day in 1943, I graduated from Tri-State College in Angola, Indiana with a Bachelor of Science Degree in Business Administration with a major in accounting. I had already received my greetings letter from Uncle Sam, but was given a deferment to complete my degree.

I had been married six months at that time to Ellen Campbell from my hometown of Bridgeport, Connecticut. We packed up and returned to Bridgeport by bus. A week later, I took the train to New Haven, Connecticut for my physical examination. My wife lived with her aunt Kit in Bridgeport where she had lived before we were married.

At the end of my physical, I was told to tell the man at the end of the line "tonsils." I didn't and I still have them sixty-two years later. Next, I was asked to choose Army or Navy. Since Bridgeport was on Long Island Sound and I swam there nearly every day each summer, I chose the Navy.

My Navy travel orders were made up and I was sent by train to Lido Beach Long Island. On the train, I met Roy Green, a friend of mine from high school days. We both graduated from Bassick High School and played sports together. After over two years in the Navy, we never saw one another again until we met on the train taking us home after our discharge from the Navy.

From Lido Beach, we boarded a troop train to upstate New York, the location of the Sampson Naval Base where I spent three months in boot camp. Since I had my college degree, they made me company clerk and because of this, I got out of many drills, mostly of the exercise variety. Our company won a competition, which gave us a day in Geneva, New York. We had our company picture taken and I looked like the biggest nerd because of the way I wore my cap, but I guess I learned how to wear it properly soon after I got out of boot camp.

While at Sampson, I received a call that my wife, Ellen, was in the hospital in Bridgeport, Connecticut and was in serious condition. The Red Cross thankfully took care of everything, my leave, transportation to Bridgeport, and return. My wife nearly died because the doctor operated on her for an ovarian cyst and gave her a local anesthetic because she had a slight cold. The anesthetic did not take and he went ahead with the operation while Ellen was screaming. My uncle visited her and thought she was going to die. He contacted the Red Cross. When I saw her, I was shocked at how weak she looked, but my visit for a few days helped her get through it. Today, that doctor would have been sued, but we were just twenty years old. We just wanted her to get well and we were happy and I returned to Sampson.

While at Sampson, I took a test for a storekeeper rating and with my degree and just graduating from college, the test seemed simple and I finished it with no problems. After waiting a week for the results, I went to the office to check. The clerk opened the drawer and quickly turned to me and said, "You didn't pass," and closed the drawer. It wasn't more than two days later that I was given my orders to report to radar training school at the Cavalier Hotel, Virginia Beach, Virginia.

This was a beautiful hotel right on the beach, but we were in classes all day long and even after dinner in the evening. Radar was new and secret. It was developed by the British. We served night radar watches from the roof of the hotel with the radar overlooking Chesapeake Bay. This school lasted a long three weeks. One of our instructors was a popular radio announce from Station WOWO, Fort Wayne, Indiana, named Bob Seivers. Later Bob was our DJ for our annual anniversary parties from our 45th to our 55th. It was around our 50th Anniversary Party that he saw pictures of me in the Navy and graduating from where he had taught. He said they were so short of books to teach from, the instructors had to pass them around.

We were warned that we could not talk about radar to anyone outside and if asked what our rating was, we would tell them radiomen because the insignia looked the same except a radar man had an arrow going through the sparks used by the radiomen insignia.

Upon completing my radar training, I was sent to Norfolk, Virginia to be assigned to a destroyer. While there, my wife Ellen joined me and we had a small apartment off base.

One day while waiting assignment, I noticed a note on the bulletin board, "Bartenders needed for Officers Club." I had worked in a liquor store during college and tended bar at fraternity parties, so I thought, what the heck, I'll apply. To my surprise, I was hired and spent three happy weeks tending bar and living with my wife in Norfolk. As a matter of fact, we had Christmas there and Ellen decorated a small tree. When I told her this was my first Christmas tree, she couldn't believe it, but it was the truth. I was raised by my grandmother and we had gifts but no tree.

A few days after Christmas 1943, I was assigned to the crew of the USS O'Brien DD725 and commenced training exercises with the crew in Norfolk. Since I could not leave the base during our training, my wife returned to Bridgeport, Connecticut and stayed with her aunt.

Upon completion of our training, we were sent by troop train to Boston, Massachusetts for our ship's commissioning. My wife and some of my relatives came up for the ceremony from Bridgeport.

I was assigned to the forward crew's quarters and chose the first bottom bunk on the starboard side with only one bunk above me and a foot locker below me. Above me was one of my radar trainees, Eugene (Red) Lambright from East Liverpool, Ohio.

The ship was built at Bath, Maine and a skeleton crew sailed her down to Boston. She was so new we had to remove some of the protective paper they used painting our lockers. It was like unwrapping our new ship.

Since I was the only schooled radar man, I trained eleven other seamen to become radar trainees, but during "General Quarters" action only five were stationed in CIC (Combat Information Center) where the radars were located.

The following was our CIC Radar crew during "General Quarters" action until the end of World War II.

Raymond P. Woods	Rdm 2/c	Wounded at Okinawa
Charles T. Conklin	Rdm 2/c	Wound at Okinawa and Cherbourg, France
John J. Deery	Rdm 2/c	Wound at Okinawa and Cherbourg, France
G. G. Codner	S 1/c	KIA Cherbourg, France
T. E. Buckley	Rdm 3/c	Wounded at Cherbourg, France and later transferred
Eugene Lambright	Rdm 2/c	Wound at Okinawa and Cherbourg, France
David (Bud) Reid	Rdm 3/c	Wounded at Okinawa

We went to sleep many nights when not on watch with the sound of the sea just inches from our heads, hitting the thin steel forward bulkhead.

CHAPTER 2

U.S.S. O'BRIEN
(DD725)

COMMISSIONING PROGRAM

NAVY YARD
Boston, Massachusetts
25 February 1944

O'BRIEN

Captain Jeremiah O'Brien and his five brothers, Gideon, John, William, Dennis and Joseph, were crew members of the sloop Unity which captured HMS Margaretta at the entrance to the harbor at Machias, Massachusetts (now Maine), 12 June 1775. Under the command of Jeremiah O'Brien, thirty-one townsmen armed with guns, swords, axes and pitchforks, captured the British armed schooner in an hour long battle after "Margaretta" had threatened to bombard the town for interference with the shipment of lumber to British troops in Boston.

I

The first O'Brien (Torpedo Boat 30) was laid down by Lewis Nixon, Elizabethport, New Jersey, 20 December 1898; launched 24 September 1900; sponsored by Miss Mira O'Brien, great-great-granddaughter of Joseph O'Brien; commissioned 15 July 1905, Lt. Edward Woods in command. Between August 1905 and April 1906, she operated with the coastal squadron between Newport and Pensacola. Placed in the Reserve Torpedo Flotilla 7 May 1906, at the Norfolk Navy Yard, she was struck from the Navy List 3 March 1909 and used as a target.

II

The second O'Brien (DD51) was laid down 8 September 1913 by William Cramp and Sons, Philadelphia; launched 20 July 1914; sponsored by Miss Marcia Bradbury Campbell, great-great-granddaughter of Gideon O'Brien; commissioned 22 May 1915, Lt. Comdr. C.E. Courtney in command.

After shakedown between Newport and Hampton Roads, she was assigned to the 5th Division, Torpedo Flotilla, Atlantic Fleet in December 1915. From early 1916 through the spring of 1917, she operated with the Fleet along the east coast and in Cuban waters.

Returning from winter maneuvers off Cuba in March 1917, the ship was in the York River when the United States entered World War I, 6 April 1917. After fitting out at Brooklyn Navy Yard, she got underway from New York 15 May 1917, and joined convoy at Halifax, Nova Scotia, enroute to Ireland. Upon arrival at Queenstown (now Cobh) 24 May 1917, she was assigned to the 6th Destroyer Division which cooperated with the British Forces. She patrolled off the Irish coast in company with other destroyers answering distress calls and meeting eastbound convoys to escort them through the war zone.

While escorting SS Elysia 12 miles off Queenstown 16 June 1917, O'Brien sighted a periscope. Heading toward the submarine for an attack, a lookout in the foretop saw the submerged boat pass close along the starboard side. A depth charge was dropped but no immediate evidence of damage was found. Nearly three hours later, the British vessel Jessamine reported a large patch of oil in approximately the same position. The next morning, Cushing Also reported and confirmed Jessamine's report. The British Admiralty believed the submarine was probably seriously damaged. However, later investigation has shown that the contact, German submarine U-16, continued to operate and completed her cruise.

In the summer of 1918, O'Brien was transferred to the French coast where she continued her antisubmarine patrol.

After the Armistice, she transported mail and passengers between Brest, France and Plymouth, England. She returned to New York 8 January 1919, and decommissioned in Philadelphia 9 June 1922. O'Brien was struck from the Navy List 8 March 1935. Scrapped at Philadelphia Navy Yard, her materials were sold 23 April 1935.

III

The third O'Brien (DD415) was laid down at Boston Navy Yard, Boston, Massachusetts, 31 May 1938; launched 20 October 1939; sponsored by Miss Josephine O'Brien Campbell, great-great-great-granddaughter of Gideon O'Brien; and commissioned 2 March 1940, Lt. Comdr. Carl F. Espe, in command. Since the ship was built in dry-dock with Walke, Landsdale and Madison, the christening ceremonies were combined.

Through 1940 and 1941, the ship operated along the eastern seaboard. After dry docking and repairs in the fall of 1941, the ship left Norfolk 15 January 1942 with Idaho and Mustin and steamed for the Pacific. Transiting the Panama Canal on the 20th, the trio arrived in San Francisco, 31 January 1942.

O'Brien sailed with a convoy for the western Pacific 4 February, but was forced to return when a collision with destroyer Cass damaged her port side. Following repairs at Mare Island, the ship sailed 20 February via San Diego, to Pearl Harbor. There Commander Destroyer Division 4 shifted his flag to O'Brien 5 March.

After operating out of Pearl Harbor and patrolling French Frigate Shoals, the ship called at Midway in the latter part of March, escorting Curtiss to evacuate civilian personnel. The two returned to Pearl on 3 April 1942. After increase and improvement of her anti-aircraft batteries, the ship embarked passengers for the Naval Air Station at Palmyra and sailed 18 April with Flusser and Mugford. The DD then joined convoys from San Diego and San Francisco escorting them to Samoa, arriving Pago Pago, 28 April.

O'Brien was retained at Pago Pago for local escort work. On 26 May, she supported the occupation of Wallis Island, previously taken over by the free French and joined Procyon 19 June for the return voyage to Pearl Harbor.

Operating out of Pearl Harbor, the ship performed escort duty and acted as patrol and plane guard. She got underway 17 August 1942 with TF 17 to reinforce the South Pacific Force, screening the oiler Guadalupe. While escorting a convoy of transports enroute to Guadalcanal, joint TFs 17 and 18 were attacked by the Japanese submarines I-15 and I-19 on 15 September 1942. Wasp was sunk; North Carolina and O'Brien were damaged by torpedo attacks.

At 1452 that afternoon, O'Brien sighted smoke coming from Wasp. As a member of Hornet's ASW screen she made an emergency turn to the right. At about 1454, while accelerating and swinging right, her lookouts spotted a torpedo two points forward off the port beam 1000 yards away. This torpedo missed close astern, but while attention was concentrated on it another "fish" hit the port bow.

The explosion did little local damage, but set up severe structural stresses through the ship. Able to proceed under her own power, the destroyer on 16 September reached Espiritu Santo, where Curtiss made temporary repairs. O'Brien sailed on the 21st for Noumea, New Calendonia, for further repairs by Argonne before proceeding on 10 October to San Francisco.

She made Suva on the 13th and sailed once more on the 16th. The rate of leaking continued to increase, and the 18th it was necessary for O'Brien to proceed to the nearest anchorage. Topside weight was jettisoned and preparations were made for abandoning ship, but it was still thought that the ship could be brought intact to Pago Pago. However, at 0600 on 19 October, the bottom suddenly opened up considerably and the forward and after portions of the hull began to work independently. At 0630 all hands, except a salvage crew went over the side; and half an hour later the ship was abandoned entirely. Just before 0800, she went under, after steaming almost 3000 miles since torpedoed. All the crew was saved.

DD415 earned 1 battle star during World War II.

IV

The fourth O'Brien (DD725) was laid down by Bath Iron Works, Bath, Maine, 8 December 1943 and launched 12 July 1943; sponsored by Miss Josephine O'Brien Campbell, great-great-great-granddaughter of Gideon O'Brien and commissioned at Boston Naval Shipyard, Comdr. P.F. Heerbrandt in command 25 February 1944.

Pictures of Several USS O'Brien Ships

USS O'Brien TB 30	USS O'Brien DD 51
USS O'Brien DD 451	USS O'Brien DD 725
USS O'Brien DD 725	USS O'Brien DD 975

USS

The Commanding Officer, Officers and Crew
request the honour of the presence of

Mrs. Raymond Wade

at the commissioning of the

U. S. S. O'Brien

at the Navy Yard, Boston, Massachusetts
on Friday, the twenty-fifth of February
nineteen hundred and forty-four
at three o'clock

Please present this card
at the Main Gate   No cameras allowed

U. S. S. O'BRIEN
(DD725)

COMMISSIONING PROGRAM

USS O'BRIEN DD725 STATISTICS

When commissioned, the fourth O'Brien DD725, had an overall length of 376 feet, 6 inches; an extreme beam of 40 feet, 10 inches; full load displacement of 3315 tons; maximum draft of 15 feet, 8 inches; and accommodations for 20 officers and 325 men. She was armed with six 5 inch/38 caliber guns, two twin and two quadruple 40-mm antiaircraft mounts and two quintuple 21 inch deck torpedo tubes. Her four Babcock and Wilcox boilers powered her two turbine engines. Her twin screws drove the ship at a maximum speed of 34.2 knots. Her contract price was $5,100,000 for hull and machinery.

COMMANDING OFFICERS – USS O'BRIEN DD725

Commander P.F. Heerbrandt, USN ....25 Feb 1944 – 29 May 1944
Commander W.W. Outerbridge, USN..............29 May 1944 - -26 Apr 1945
Commander I.B. Gragg, USN........................26 April 1945 – 19 Oct 1045
Commander H.E. Day, USN...........................19 Oct 1945 – 26 Apr 1947
Lt. Commander O.F. Dreyer, USN ....26 Apr 1947 – 8 Jul 1947
Lt. Commander J.P. Rizza, Jr., USN ....8 Jul 1947 – 2 Sep 1947
Lieutenant George T. Weir, USN ....2 Sep 1947 – 4 Oct 1947
Commander C.W. Nimitz, Jr., USN ....5 Oct 1950 – 21 Dec 1951
Commander F.G. Dierman, USN......................21 Dec 1951 – 29 Jan 1954
Commander T.A. Melusky, USN.........................29 Jan 1954 – 17 Jun 1955
Commander F.W. Deily, USN ....17 Jun 1955 – 29 Oct 1956
Commander O.E. Gray, Jr., USN....................29 Oct 1956 – 13 Sep 1958

USS O'BRIEN – DD-725
AERIAL 3/4 BOW VIEW, UNDERWAY. 18 MARCH, 1944

Midship Looking Forward - Starboard Side

From Mount #3 Looking Forward

Priest - Cleaning Gun

Portside Forward - (?)

1945

Main 5" Battery Direcon
and Score Board

Grady and Slattery
Tailor Made Uniforms

We left Boston for our first shakedown cruise right after commissioning the sleek speed of the O'Brien combined with day and night land bombardment, night torpedo boat attacks, practice anti-submarine searches and attacks with the plotting done in the combat information center which was our Radar Room and aircraft firing practice at sleeves, pulled by our planes were some very new and exciting moments and days for me.

These cruises made our ship a team and the more we practiced, the more accurate we became, and the crew became proud of their accomplishments and their ship.

During our shakedown cruise off Bermuda, we got one day liberty in beautiful Hamilton, Bermuda. Although I didn't understand the British money, I was able to buy a dress for my wife and sent it to her from there. She was not only surprised to receive it, but that it did fit.

On our return trip to Boston from Bermuda, we made a night speed run and, if I remember correctly, we went over 36 knots, which is over 40 miles per hour. On water, it seemed as if we were flying.

The speed run was made at night. I had a weird feeling because the night was dark and moonless and of the stories that had been told about planes and ships that had known to disappear in the Bermuda Triangle.

Back in Boston, we spent a short time making corrections and improvements to the ship that were discovered were needed during our shakedown cruise.

CHAPTER 3

Next, we left Boston for New York City and had an enjoyable six hour liberty until midnight. As we were walking down the dock returning from our liberty, we saw that the O'Brien had steam up and was ready to leave the dock.

We knew now that we were going to be heading for action.

We shoved off a little after midnight and joined outside of New York with (8) Ammunition Ships and our destroyer division. Our destroyer division consisted of (5) new 2200 ton destroyers the same class as the O'Brien. Destroyer Division 119 consisted of the USS Barton DD722, USS Walke DD723, USS Laffey DD724, USS O'Brien DD725 and the USS Meredith DD726.

We crossed the North Atlantic without incident and docked at Belfast, Ireland. I had a short liberty in Belfast and went to a very first class restaurant. The waiters were dressed in tuxedos, the tables had linen tablecloths and napkins. I was alone and feeling strange as I looked at the menu. There were very few items on the menu so I ordered the Welsh Rarebit. What a shock to find I had ordered melted cheese on toast along with the grayest cup of coffee I had ever seen.

The O'Brien left Belfast alone and we sailed down the Irish Sea close to the Irish shore. The weather was beautiful and with the heather growing on sides of the beautiful green hills, being of Irish decent, I was thrilled at seeing that much of Ireland.

We then sailed around the southern tip of England and into the harbor at Plymouth, England. Barrage balloons flew over the harbor and the docks were crowded with fighting ships. We tied up to another destroyer but there were about five or six ships we had to go through to get to the dock, but at this time there were no men leaving the ship with perhaps the exception of the captain. Because of the rush, our convoy left from New York and the type of ships we escorted we told some of the sailors on the other ships the invasion will be very soon now. They laughed at us and told us how long they had been there and hearing the same story.

We were right because I don't believe it was more than two days later we were ordered to sea on June 4th. When we got out into the English Channel, the waves were wild and impossible for the smaller ships to sail. We were ordered to return to Portland overnight.

We set out the next day and joined 45 LCI's loaded with troops and our job was to lead these ships safely across the channel to Utah Beach. This we did with the exception of one incident at about mid channel, we picked up a sonar contact and dropped depth charges on the contact and stayed with it until we lost contact.

We then raced back to the front of our 45 LCI's and continued across the channel. We arrived with all 45 LCI's at Utah Beach about 7:00 a.m.

Years later back in Bridgeport, Connecticut, I met one of the soldiers that was on one of the LCI's and he told me the story about the destroyer that was leading them across the channel; it broke off and fired depth charges all over the place. He said you can imagine the feeling of those soldiers, watching this action and we were only at mid channel. He was surprised when I told him I was on that destroyer.

Most of that night, the sky was covered with planes and gliders heading for the French coast. The first tracer fire we saw was about 3:00 a.m. coming from the French coast. After leaving the LCI's at Utah Beach at 7:22 a.m. June 6, 1944, we rushed up to Omaha Beach. On our trip to Omaha, we watched the initial bombardment battleships, cruisers and destroyers much of it was wasted on Pointe du Hoe, where the Germans had removed their guns from the huge emplacement before D-Day.

We reached our standby location between 8:30 and 9:00 a.m. We were about 4000 yards off Omaha Beach. There we watched the annihilation of the first wave. Bodies were floating in the water throughout the beach. We then watched the second wave try to land some landing craft, were hit, and some turned away from the heavy fire going in circles. This went on until sometime after 9:00 a.m. when our skipper, W.W. Outerbridge, took it upon himself, without orders, to head the O'Brien straight toward the beach and the cliffs near Omaha Beach. At about 500 yards, the captain swung the O'Brien hard right parallel with the cliffs and began firing all our six 5" guns at the top of the cliffs where the pillboxes and machine guns were located.

I was told later that two other destroyers did the same thing without orders. After our first salvo, we heard radio cries from the cliffs. It was our own men the Rangers who had made it to the bottom of the cliffs but could not move being pinned down by the German guns above. Our skipper asked over the radio "Did we hurt anyone?" The answer came back quickly "No, but raise your fire a little." The reason I knew this was the fact that I was monitoring the radio in our Radar Room at the time. It was also the reason the captain stopped and backed up the O'Brien.

We did raise our fire and moved right up the beach delivering salvo after salvo at the top of the cliffs. As we reached a point near Point du Hoe, we saw German soldiers running from the cliffs to a lone building that was set back from the beach. The captain waited until the Germans entered the building then he gave orders to destroy it. We did with one salvo.

I would like to mention now that during the 50th Anniversary of D-Day, A&E Television had a program about D-Day and interviewed several men that were there. One of the officers described what our ship, the O'Brien, did that day exactly and commented that at least where he was that was the turning point of the invasion. He also ended his comment saying, "Thank God for the US Navy."

In looking at our ship's log enclosed for D-Day, no mention was made of our moving in toward the cliffs north of Point du Hoe between 9:00 a.m. and noon. It is my opinion since the O'Brien moved in to blast the German pillboxes and machine gun nests without orders, the captain had them kept off our log thus A.B. Feber's story about the O'Brien entitled "Born to Fight the USS O'Brien" in the magazine "Destroyers at War" dated our bombardment June 7th, not June 6th as was the fact. His article even speaks of the enemy soldiers running from the last pillbox the O'Brien hit and I saw them run to the only building just a slight distance in from the shore. After they were in the building, the captain ordered it destroyed. I have always felt that the O'Brien and Captain Outerbridge never got the credit they deserved from our work on D-Day, June 6th, not June 7th.

The following quotes were taken from men who were on the beach when the O'Brien attacked the guns on the cliffs west of Omaha Beach on D-Day. They can be found in Stephen Ambrose's book called "D-Day."

Seaman Giguene was on the beach when he states, "A destroyer came in as close to shore as could be. She was firing at a pillbox just over my head. It was a funny feeling hearing the shells go over my head." Seaman O'Neil, also on the beach, recalled "The destroyers were firing their 5" shells point blank at the pillboxes; you could see the shells as they went screaming overhead and smacked against the thick concrete walls. They bounced skyward off the sloping sides of the pillboxes, but they managed to get a few of them in the gun ports. The enemy fire soon stopped."

Lt. Joe Smith, a Navy beach master, remembered seeing "The destroyers come right into the beach firing into the cliff. You could see the trenches, guns and men blowing up where they would hit. They aimed right below the edge of the cliffs where the trenches were dug in. There is no question in my mind that the few Navy destroyers that we had there saved the invasion." In his conclusion, Smith spoke for every man who witnessed the scene: "Believe me I was a destroyer man from that day on."

James Knight, an Army engineer on a demolition team who landed at 6:30 a.m. at Fox Red said that he had been pinned down until about 10:00 a.m., "A destroyer loomed out of the sea...headed straight toward me. Even though she wasn't listing or smoking, my first thought was that she had either struck a mine or taken a torpedo and was damaged badly enough that she was being beached."

But the destroyer began to turn right. Before she was parallel to the beach she was blazing away with all her guns. Shells landed just a few feet over Knight's head. He watched her proceed westward along the beach, firing constantly. He expected to see her pull out to sea at any moment "when suddenly I realized she was backing up and her guns had yet to pause. She backed up almost to where she had started, went dead in the water for the second time…and again headed toward the other end of the beach with all guns still blazing." Knight has been trying to find out that ship's name for years after the war. It sounds to me exactly what the USS O'Brien DD725 did on D-Day. It will probably never be known unless someone reads this.

Admiral Morrison got it right when he wrote, "The destroyer action against shore batteries afforded the troops the only artillery support they had during most of D-Day. The cruisers and battleships, unable to go in close, were banging away at major emplacements on the cliff east and west of Omaha whose position was known before the invasion and with good effect, but the troops ashore could neither see nor sense the results. But the effect on the troops on Omaha of the destroyer's heroic and risky action was electric."

At the time I wrote this I was confused because my copy of the ship's log signed by the officers said we patrolled Utah Beach until midnight. In May 2012, I obtained a copy of the recently released government "War Diary, USS O'Brien, June 1944-March 1945." This diary leaves out all the action we on the O'Brien faced June 6th by conveniently eliminating a ship's log entry from 0720 a.m. as we landed the troops at Utah Beach until 2157 p.m. when it says we moved out of the patrol section to Omaha Beach. This eliminates everything that I say happened on June 6th D-Day on pages here in this book.

In addition, I have a copy of **our ship's log** for that day and it doesn't agree with the War Diary. Our officers signed off that we stayed patrolling at Utah Beach until midnight. What actually happened and covered in my book after dropping the LCI's at Utah Beach about 0750 a.m. June 6th D-Day we then rushed alone up to Omaho Beach arriving and anchoring off Omaha Beach at about 0830 a.m. after which we saw the action described in this book (see copy of logs attached).

I have had two occasions during my lifetime to wonder what was going on. In 1949 Lonas Frey, a former shipmate on the O'Brien, gave me a copy of a magazine article about the O'Brien in "Destroyers at War" the name of the article was "Born to Fight: The USS O'Brien." They were interviewing our ex-officer Lt. Commander K.G. Robinson. He was an officer friend who was the only person with me to escape from the radar room uninjured when the O'Brien was hit by a large German Shore Battery on June 25th at Cherbourg, France. Although two officers and four enlisted men were wounded and one enlisted man was killed, Robinson said the O'Brien stayed the rest of the day, June 6th, patrolling at Utah Beach which is not true.

The other occasion was in the 1970's while I was working for St. Rita's Medical Center in Lima, Ohio. I was at a meeting in Cincinnati, Ohio at the Sisters of Mercy home office and met Mr. Robinson, who was working for one of their colleges. When he saw me, he barely waved and disappeared from the meeting. I thought that was funny after our association on the O'Brien. As a matter of fact, when we were going through the escape hatch at Cherbourg he said, "Well, we are on our second one now, Ray."

After giving a great deal of thought as to the reason the records were made to show the O'Brien was not at Omaha Beach on D-Day, I've concluded this. Our captain, Commander W.W. Outerbridge, was a career Navy officer and had already been credited with firing the first shot of WWII against Japan when as captain of the destroyer USS Ward he sank a midget Japanese submarine on the entrance to Pearl Harbor before the Jap planes attacked. The sub was later brought to the surface and had a five inch hole in the conning tower. Captain Outerbridge would never do anything to hurt his Naval career.

When the O'Brien left the LCI's at Utah Beach it was 7:50 a.m. on June 6th. The first wave of our troops attacked Omaha Beach at 6:30 a.m. June 6th. I think that the captain had been listening to the reports of the carnage at Omaha Beach. He took it upon himself to rush up to Omaha Beach without orders since it was just about a half-hour from Utah Beach. Since he did not have orders to go to Omaha Beach, he could not let it be known what the O'Brien did that day. After the captain observed the carnage on the beach and the second wave being turned back, he took the O'Brien into attack the guns that were wiping out our troops. These guns were in a tunnel at the top of a cliff at Red Beach.

It's no wonder that James Knight, the Army Engineer that was on the shore and described exactly what the O'Brien did, could not find the name of our ship for years after the war when you think of all the lives that were saved by our ship's action and since the War Diary showed that the O'Brien's orders were to report to the Commander Destroyer Div. 36 in the USS Harding the morning of June 7th at Omaha Beach for shore bombardment.

I now feel our captain Commander W.W. Outerbridge should be commended not criticized for what he did. He had foresight and initiative to take action at a time when it was badly needed and no orders were being given. After we attacked the German guns the other two destroyers went into action and then orders were sent out to all destroyers, "Go get them boys. They are hurting our troops."

The results of Captain Outerbridge's action machine gun firing from the tunnel ceased and I believe the big guns that were hidden three miles inland were silenced because they were probably getting their target coordinates from the tunnel. This conclusion was reached when I read a story about how one of our soldiers discovered the guns hidden behind a farmhouse. He was able to disable the guns because their gun crews were talking up on a road away from the guns. They could have been talking about why they weren't getting anymore targets from the tunnel at Omaha Beach.

After the bombardment D-Day afternoon quieted down for the O'Brien; we patrolled the beach until between twelve midnight and 1:00 a.m. I was operating our SC Aircraft Radar and picked up a contact at 100 miles. Because of the distance, I thought it might be the whole German Air force, but as I watched the images close on the screen, the back of the images began to fade.

Remembering my schooling at Virginia Beach, I suspected the Germans were using jamming, done by dropping foil. I still did not know the number of planes approaching. It turned out to be just one Junker German Bomber.

Orders were given to all ships to hold their fire. The next thing I heard was two loud blasts and the O'Brien rocked. I called the bridge and asked what we were firing at. The answer came back, "Firing? Hell, we've been bombed!" Although this is hard to believe, the next night at almost the same time, the same thing happened again. This German Junker Bomber laid a string of 250 lb. bombs up the starboard side of the O'Brien. The ship leaned right about 45 degrees and then righted itself. I didn't have to call the bridge this time; I knew what happened. We had been bombed again.

For years, I could not figure out why, with all the ships lying off Omaha Beach, the O'Brien was picked out and bombed two nights in a row by possibly the same German Bomber. Some time later, I was talking to Lonas (Lonnie) Frey who manned a 20mm anti-aircraft gun on the fantail of the O'Brien at Omaha. Lonnie was from a neighboring town to my hometown of Ottawa, Ohio. He was from Pandora, Ohio and we met again as members of the Ottawa, Ohio VFW Post 9142. I asked him, "Did we have any light showing or why were we picked out as a target?" He said that the German Bomber dropped flares and it was like daylight out there. The O'Brien, being a new 2200 ton destroyer, looked like a cruiser to them and an excellent target. This finally settled my worry for the rest of WWII that we might have a light showing from above our ship at night making us a target for night air attacks.

CHAPTER 4

After patrolling the beach at Omaha for several days, we were ordered back to England. It was just to pick up supplies, ammunition, and mail for the fleet. While in Plymouth, two things happened to us that we will remember. We went to a theatre and sat behind some British ladies. To our surprise, the Movietone News came on the screen showing Omaha Beach and we began to talk to ourselves about what was being shown. One of the ladies in front of us turned and told us we should be ashamed of ourselves and feel sorry for the boys over there. We admired the British so much that we didn't tell them we just came from there and were going back the next day. In looking back, I wish we had explained to those women in the theatre that we were talking during the news because of the relief we felt watching that film about Omaha Beach and not being there at the moment, but knowing we were going back over there the next day.

The other incident was when we were invited to dinner at a British family's apartment. We arrived and opened the front door to go upstairs to their apartment, and we were looking up at the open sky. The building had been bombed and still not repaired. We did bring some staples from our ship and gave them to the family who wanted to share the little they had with us.

After returning to Omaha Beach, we delivered mail to several ships and continued to patrol. On approximately June 24, 1944, we were ordered again to return to England. Everyone was happy because it probably meant we were through here and to return to Boston. Our happiness was short lived when the whole crew was called out at midnight to help load ammunition and supplies.

On June 25, 1944, we crossed the channel following mine sweepers toward the city of Cherbourg, France. At 10:30 a.m., accompanied by the battleships Texas and Arkansas, and by the destroyer's O'Brien, Barton, Laffey, Hobson and Plunkett attacked one side of Cherbourg and a like force of the USS Nevada, Cruisers Tuscalousa, Quincy, HMS Glasgow, HMS Enterprise and six American Destroyers attacked the other side of the city. The plan was to hit these targets for 90 minutes under command of Admiral Deyo on directions from General Collins.

The German guns were many, big and accurate. The battleship Texas was firing over our heads and was hit. The O'Brien pulled out of the bombardment long enough to make smoke to protect the Texas. We then returned to the bombardment and the fire of our three destroyers was hurting them so much that they stopped firing at the Texas and turned all their fire power on us. That's when the Laffey and Barton both took hits with duds that did not explode. The O'Brien wasn't as lucky and was hit and sent the following radiogram.

"This spotting station was hidden among a group of small buildings – one of which had a very strong light which was beamed toward each ship that was taken under fire. In addition, there was a house with a sloping roof that had three windows, which also contained bright lamps. During the time that the O'Brien was under attack, these lights were trained on the ship."

After being hit by a German shore battery in the bombardment of Cherbourg, Lt. Commander Robinson and I were the only ones to get out of the CIC radar room without a scratch. Of the three officers and five enlisted men in the room, one enlisted man, Bill Codner from Cleveland, Ohio, was killed and two officers and three enlisted men were wounded. As we went through the escape hatch, Commander Robinson said, "Well, Ray, we're on our second one." I didn't know what he meant at the time but I guess he was referring to a cat having nine lives; we just used one of them.

Commander Robinson went on up to help the Captain on the bridge but I was outside on deck with nothing to do except watch the shelling and the many German shells hitting the water around us. Not knowing what to do, I decided to walk from one side of the ship to the other through a central passageway always going to the side of the ship away from the side we were bombarding. I figured if we did get hit again, I would have as much steel as possible between me and the incoming shells. Fortunately, it worked because we didn't get hit again.

After the battle, Captain Outerbridge looked into the radar room and gave every enlisted man that got out of that room alive an advancement in rating. Thus I was now Rdm 3/c. "There is a possibility that the Germans have perfected a method of ranging by light. It is thought that the near perfect salvos from the shore-based artillery were due to a fire control and spotting station located about 1500 yards closer to the beach – and on a lower level to the west of the gun batteries."

Deck Log

COMMANDER DESTROYER SQUADRON 60

Heading:

- A - D725 25L545 9JG2 GR (UNKNOWN)

13 DEAD

7 WOUNDED

5 REQUIRE HOSPITALIZATION

STBD FWD 40 MM TWIN OUT OF ACTION- STBD SEARCHLIGHT DAMAGED
ALL RADARS OUT OF ACTION - CIC OUT OF ACTION - MAIN BATTERY IN
COMMISSION USING DIRECTOR AND SETREO RANGEFINDER - ALL OTHER
ARMAMENT IN COMMISSION - BRIDGE SUPERSTRUCTURE AND NO. 1 STACK
DAMAGED//.....

WU LINN/

From: U.S.S. O'BRIEN (DD725)	Date: 25 JUNE 44	Originated by:	Released by:
Action To: CTC 129.2	Deferred / Routine / Priority	Radio / Visual / Mailgm.	Restricted / Confidential / Secret

COMMANDER DESTROYER SQUADRON 60

Heading:

- A - SQUAD D60 251915B D 725 GR 53 BT

SQUADRON COMMANDER AND HIS STAFF REGRET EXTREMELY THE PASSING
OF THEIR SHIPMATES IN THE O'BRIEN TODAY AND OFFER THE CREW OF
THE O'BRIEN THEIR SINCERE SYMPATHY AS WELL AS THEIR BEST WISHES
TO THE WOUNDED SHIPMATES FOR A QUICK RECOVERY AAA WE TAKE PRIDE
IN KNOWING THAT IRISH CAN TAKE IT AND STILL FIGHT BT.....

WU LINN/

From: COMDESRON 60	Date: 6/25/44	Originated by:	Released by:
Action To: U.S.S. O'BRIEN (IRISH) 30	Deferred / Routine / Priority	Radio / Visual / Mailgm.	Restricted / Confidential / Secret

COMMANDER DESTROYER SQUADRON 60

Destroyer Force 71

Heading: -A- DIV BAT 5 25L54Ø SQUAD D6Ø CR 62 BT

PLEASE PASS TO ALL DESTROYERS WITH YOU AAA YOUR CONDUCT TODAY
HAS BEEN EXEMPLARY AAA WERE IT NOT FOR YOUR PROMPT ASSISTANCE
IN COVERING US AT CRUCIAL MOMENTS WE WOULD HAVE BEEN SEVERLY
DAMAGED AAA THE BATTERIES FIRING AT US WERE PARTICULARY ACCURATE
AND POWERFUL YET NONE OF YOU FLINCHED AAA IN FACT YOU WERE
WILLING TO PRESS HOME THE ATTACK- WELL DONE TO YOU ALL BT.....

WU LINN/

From: COMBATDIV5	Date: 6/15/44	Originated by:	Released by:
Action To: ALL DESTROYERS	Deferred / Routine / Priority	Radio / Visual / Mailgm	Restricted / Confidential / Secret

COMMANDER DESTROYER SQUADRON 60

Destroyer Force 71

Heading: - A - ØJG9 251898 JG9 GR 45 BT

THOUGH BADLY HANDICAPPED BY POOR SPOTTING CONDITIONS ASHORE
AND SERIOUSLY THREATENED BY EFFICENT ENEMY BATTERIES YOU GAVE
A FINE PERFORMANCE OF GREATEST VALUE TO THE ARMY AT A CRITICAL
TIME. THE DESTROYERS WERE PARTICULARLY RESOURCEFUL AND BOLD.
ALL SHIPS DID THEIR DUTY. WELL DONE.

CONFIDENTIAL — PAGE *125*

DECK LOG—REMARKS SHEET

UNITED STATES SHIP O'BRIEN (DD725) — Sunday 25 June 1944

0-4

Anchored outside the breakwater in Portland, England in 11 fathoms of water with 45 fathoms of chain on deck. Bearings: steeple 300 degrees T, breakwater light 280 degrees T, south breakwater light 225 degrees T, with boilers 3 & 4 in use, condition of readiness 3, material condition Baker. ComTaskGroup CTU 129. 0900 Underway steaming various courses and speeds with the Captain at the conn and the Navigator on the bridge, proceeding out south swept channel from Portland, England.

R.F. ____
Ensign, USN.

4-8

Steaming as before. 0420 Secured special sea details. 0500 Joined TG 129.2 and took station on port bow 500 yards distance from USS TEXAS, CTU 129.2 and guide in that ship. Ships of Task Group USS TEXAS, ARKANSAS, BARTON, LAFFEY, PLUNKETT, HOBSON, and this ship. 0530 Steadied on base course 107 degrees T, 106 degrees PGC, 120 degrees PSC at speed 15 knots. 0600 Lighted ship.

J.F. ____
Lieut., USNR.

8-12

Steaming as before. 0800 Mustered the crew on stations - no absentees. Made daily inspection of magazines and smokeless powder samples - conditions normal. 0905 c/o to 149 degrees T, 170 degrees PGC, 179 degrees PSC. 0930 Went to general quarters and set material condition Able. 0946 c/o to 18 knots. 0950 Arrived in firing area and commenced steering various courses at various speeds conforming to the swept channel. 1022 Commenced acting as fire support ship for minesweeping unit Two, steering various courses at various speeds off Cherbourg, France.

E.J. ____
Lieut., USNR.

12-16

Steaming as before. 1205 USS ARKANSAS opened fire on German shore batteries on Cherbourg, peninsula. 1233 This ship commenced firing salvo fire at shore batteries bearing 221 degrees T, distance 9800 yards. 1245 This ships fire falling in area of enemy gun flashes. 1255 Hit by enemy shell from shore battery, on starboard side of signal bridge, putting number one 40mm mount out of action, both flagbags destroyed, CIC and searchhand surface radars out of action. The following named men were killed in action: _____ ... Making turns for 27 knots and steering northeast to clear minesweepers. 1312 Ceased firing. 1400 Falling in astern of USS BARTON, steering various courses at various speeds, screening USS ARKANSAS and USS TEXAS. 1417 Unloaded guns through muzzle. Total rounds expended 193 rounds AA common 5"/38.

J.F. ____
Lieut., USNR.

16-20

Steaming as before. 1601 Enroute Cherbourg to Portland, England screening on port bow of USS TEXAS, 1500 yards, course 351 degrees T, 350 degrees PGC, speed 15 knots. 1605 c/o to 300 degrees PGC. 1615 Base course 290 degrees PGC, 291 degrees T. 1630 Secured from general quarters, set condition 3. 1713 c/o to 001 degrees T, 000 degrees PGC. 1832 c/o to 331 degrees PGC, 330 degrees T. 1840 c/o to 278 degrees T, 277 degrees PGC. 1900 Mustered all hands. 13 known dead, none missing.

J.F. ____
Lieut., USNR.

20-24

Steaming as before. 2007 c/o to 313 degrees T, 312 degrees PGC. 2036 c/o to 276 degrees T, 277 degrees PGC. 2109 Steering various courses at various speeds conforming to channel to Portland, England. 2224 Moored starboard side to USS MELVILLE, with following lines out and doubled: 1, 2, 3, 4, 5, & 6. 2243 USS LAFFEY moored alongside to port. 2245 USS BARTON moored to port side of LAFFEY. 2330 All hands to quarters for muster - Absentees: 13 known dead.

J.F. ____
Lieut., USNR.

APPROVED: ____   EXAMINED: ____

- 9b -

____ Lieut.Comdr., USN

CONFIDENTIAL   PAGE __10__

DECK LOG—REMARKS SHEET

UNITED STATES SHIP ___O'BRIEN (DD725)___   Tuesday   6   June   19 44

0-4

Steaming on course 130 degrees T 129 PGC enroute Plymouth to Northern coast of France, Baie de la Seine, as USS of Naval Commander Western Task Force's invasion armada, in company with and screening flotilla of 45 LCI's, convoy section U1B. Convoy guide is LCI 217. Convoy Commodore Commander J. B. Brennan, U.S.C.G. in LCI 381. Screen commander commanding, Commanding Officer this ship. Wing escorts TAM 366 & 347, SC 1330 & 1334. Salcombe, Dartmouth and Torquay sections of LCI's included in convoy. Standard speed fifteen knots, steaming at sixteen on boilers # & 4, # & 5 on standby. Acting in accordance with ComTaskForce 2 operation order 3-44 and Naval Commander Western Task Force's 040859B. This ship at General Quarters with condition of readiness 1 and material condition 'A' set. Ship darkened. 0012 c/s to 138 degrees T, 109 PGC. 0037 c/s to 070 degrees T. 0118 c/s to 9 knots.

           J. P. Murphy
           Lieut., USNR.

4-8

Steaming as before. 0430 Changed speed to 12 knots. 0503 Passed buoy Jig and entered swept channel leading to Utah beach area of the western invasion forces in the Baie De La Seine and commenced steering various courses at various speeds conforming to the channel. 0430 British and U. S. Forces commenced landing on the northern coast of France in the Baie De La Seine. Various units of the U. S. Naval and British naval forces supported the landing operations and laid a smoke screen. 0722 Convoy U1B left the escort of this ship and proceeded toward the beach. U.S.S. O'BRIEN took screening station southward of transports to south east in anchorage in accordance with CTF 125 top secret operation XXXXXX.

   O'Brien rushed from UTAH Beach To Omaha Beach
   rushed off Omaha Beach for fire Support

           E. J. Dougherty
           Lieut., USNR.

8-12

Steaming as before. 0800 Made daily inspection of magazines and smokeless powder samples. Conditions normal.

   Opened fire on pillbox at Omaha Beach

           J. P. Murphy
           Lieut., USNR.

12-16

Steaming as before. 1207 Changed screening station to northward of transport area, distance about four thousand yards.

           E. J. Dougherty
           Lieut., USNR.

16-20

Steaming as before.

           J. P. Murphy
           Lieut., USNR.

20-24

Steaming as before. 2733 Anchored in area (C) 47 Baie De La Seine, France in 10 fathoms of water with 30 fathoms of chain out to the port anchor.

           E. J. Dougherty
           Lieut., USNR.

APPROVED:

           - 9c -

DD725

U. S. S. O'BRIEN

Serial 056

Subject: War Diary30 June 1944

- -- - - - - - - - - - - - -

June		
6 – (Cont'd)	0000	screen showed few planes on bearing 140T, Range 20,000 yards not closing this convoy. Night action believed to be friendly patrol vessels engaging "snoooper" aircraft.
	0330	Passed Convoy U-3 abeam to port distance about 1000 yards. U.S.S. MEREDITH was escorting this convoy.
	0503	Entered Swept Channel 1, proceeding to transport area.
	0720	Passed Point K, Red and Green LCI groups proceeded to assigned areas. Arrived at transport area at H hour plus 50 minutes. Ten minutes ahead of scheduled time of arrival. No stragglers or casualties enroute. This convoy passed all navigational markers in accordance with the prearranged plan. Squadron Commanders of the LCI Squadrons kept their ships closed up and in position. U.S.S. O'BRIEN proceeded to Sector southeast of transport area and commenced A/S patrol on various courses at various speeds as previously directed.
	2157	Shifted patrol sector to area southeast of Red LCT anchorage.
	2233	Anchored in 10 fathoms of water on patrol station 4000 yards southeast of LCT anchorage.
June 7	0640	Anchored as before. Underway proceeding to area off Chateau de la Barren to report to Commander Destroyer Division 36 in U.S.S. Harding FOR SHORE BOMBARDMENT.
	1013	Commenced firing on German pill box (coordinates 585964), Chateau de la Barren, Normandy, France, as directed by U.S. Army Ranger Fire Control Party #1. Opened fire at range 2850 yards – fired only one salvo.
	1014	Ceased firing as directed by shore fire control group, having expended six rounds 5" /38 caliber AA Common ammunition.

Charleston Navy Yard, Boston. Commander Outerbridge awarding Purple Heart to the wounded at Cherbourg, France — 9 August 1944.

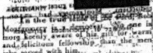

"A Typical Fighting American"

...had ...

In the ... of the ...
Montgomery in ... No one is more keenly aware of his gift for warm and felicitous fellowship than the men who served with him.

When he was stationed at Boston a few months before the Normandy invasion, in which he was to take part, he struck up a friendship with an enlisted man, a young signalman on his ship. Geographically and in most other ways they had little in common. The sailor had been born in Italy; he had grown up in ... circles about Boston ... no container and scantily Ameri-

... and he had a daughter named Eliza-beth. So had Bob.

The bond grew into hero-worship on the sailor's part. When they were off duty, he would volunteer to drive Montgomery about the city, and one day shyly invited Bob to visit his parents. Bob went to see them in their modest quarters over a store. He made himself a part of the family.

Then orders came to put to sea, and when the destroyer squadron arrived in England, Bob was transferred from his ship, the O'Brien, to another destroyer, but his and the O'Brien's vessels were close together when the flotilla set forth across the channel on the fateful day of the invasion. They were close enough so that Bob, through his glasses, could see his friend in the crow's-nest—so close that he could see the shell-burst that ended the life of his friend.

Three weeks later, when the squadron was safely back at an English port, ... that services were held on the O'B., as, for the loss, she lost in the engagement. The commodore, who knew of the friendship between the lieutenant commander and the Italian-born Boston boy, asked Bob to say a few words.

Bob has no record of what he said, and probably he wouldn't repeat the words if he remembered them. He does remember, though, that the services for the twelve killed on the O'Brien were held in the compartment below deck, before an altar at half-draped ... which the chaplain had improvised.

He recounted this episode recently at an off-the-record talk he gave at a press-club meeting in Hollywood, and it is by his permission that it now appears for the first time in print. His purpose in telling the story to the press club was not to extol himself, but to pay tribute to his friend, which he did at the end of his talk with these words: "Here was a boy, born in Italy and raised in America, who gave his life in the liberation of a coun-try he had never set foot on, and who now was buried in England—a typical fight-

Allied Fleet Hit Cherbourg For 3½ Hours

3 U. S. Battle-ships and 2 Cruisers, With 5 British Vessels, Under American

By Ned Russell

By Telephone to the Herald Tribune

Copyright, 1944, New York Tribune Inc.

SUPREME HEADQUARTERS, Allied Expeditionary Force, June 25.—American and British warships bombarded Cherbourg for three and a half hours yesterday, it was disclosed tonight.

The task force, which included three American battleships, two American cruisers and four American destroyers, as well as two British cruisers and three British destroyers, plus British and American flotillas of mine sweepers, fought a series of gun duels with German shore batteries.

As the battle progressed the warships edged closer to shore, some going within 3,000 yards of the port.

An official summary of the action indicated that the counter-shelling from the shore batteries had been stronger than anticipated. No announcement was made about damage or casualties to the Allied forces.

The report disclosed that the American commander of the task forces, Rear Admiral Morton L. Deyo, of Kittery Point, Me., flying his flag in the heavy cruiser Tuscaloosa, had planned to shell the port's targets for ninety minutes and then withdraw, but stayed on for another two hours to "remove further obstacles from the path of the army."

American ships in the ...

LOCATION: BAIE DE LA SEINE AND CHERBOURG PENINSULA

TIME: 6 JUNE 10 1 JULY 1944

MSC. JUNE 30, 1944

FROM: ADMIRAL DEYO
TO: ASSAULT SCREEN AND CHERBOURG TASK FORCE

UPON YOUR DEPARTURE FROM THE WESTERN NAVAL TASK FORCE FOR OTHER
DUTY, I SEND TO YOU ALL, YOUR OFFICERS AND MEN, MY HEARTIEST CONGRATULA-
TIONS ON THE RECORD YOU HAVE MADE IN THIS THEATRE. THE ACCURACY AND
POWER OF YOUR GUNFIRE SUPPORT MADE A DECISIVE
CONTRIBUTION TO THE INITIAL ASSAULT AND THE ADVANCE INLAND. YOUR ESCORT-
ING AND PROTECTIVE DUTIES HAVE BEEN HANDLED WITH GREAT SKILL. THE BOLD
AND VIOLENT ATTACK UPON THE CHERBOURG DEFENSES WAS A FITTING CLIMAX TO
YOUR VISIT TO FRANCE. IT HAS BEEN AN HONOR TO COMMAND SUCH SHIPS AS
YOURS AND IN YOUR FUTURE OPERATIONS I CAN WISH YOU NO BETTER LUCK THAN
THAT WILL TO UPHOLD THE
STANDARDS YOU HAVE SET IN THE BATTLE OF NORMANDY.

WU-CR

From: ADMIRAL DEYO   Date 7/5/44

Action To: ASSAULT SCREEN AND CHERBOURG
              TASK FORCE

- A - SQUAD D60 1913368 DDIV 119 GR 93 BT-

ON JUNE EIGHTEEN COMDESRON SIXTY INSPECTED BEACH AREA AND SECTIONS
BEHIND BEACH INCLUDING A NUMBER OF TARGETS WHICH WERE FIRED ON BY
SHIPS OF DESDIN ONE NINETEEN X THE FIRE SUPPORT RENDERED WAS VERY
EFFECTIVE AS INDICATED BY THE DESTRUCTION OBSERVED AND STATEMENTS
OF BOTH ARMY AND NAVY PERSONNEL WHO WERE INVOLVED IN OPERATIONS
ASHORE X CONVEY THIS INFORMATION TO YOUR ENTIRE CREWS INCLUDING
MY PERSONNEL GRATULATIONS OF THEIR EXCELLENT PERFORMANCE IN
ASSISTING OUR LAND FORCES IN CLEARING AND SECURING THE BEACHHEAD
IN THE MOST COMPLICATED AND EXTENSIVE AMPHIBIOUS OPERATION EVER
UNDERTAKEN BT......

WU LINN/VIA BRIDGE

From: COMDESRON 60   Date: 6/19/44

Action To: DESDIV 119

Reset from original

Upon our return to England, we transferred our dead and left England alone to cross the rough North Atlantic with no radar or sonar. We arrived at Boston's Charlestown Navy Yard where we were commissioned less then five months earlier.

The crew was given thirty day leave while the ship was under repair. It took 300,000 man hours to repair the O'Brien. It was about August, 1944 that we left Boston and accompanied a carrier through the Panama Canal to San Diego. While going through the Panama Canal, we docked at Balboa, Canal Zone and had a six hour liberty. It was hot and one of my buddies and I stopped at a bar to cool off, but with rum and cokes fifteen cents, we stayed much too long and ended up in the local jail until we came to and were returned to our ship by the Shore Patrol in a jeep. My punishment for this bit of fun was that I lost my advancement to Rdm 2/c which was about due - so much for fun in Panama.

CHAPTER 5

We then left San Diego for Pearl Harbor where our Captain W.W. Outerbridge fired the first shot of World War II as captain of the Destroyer Ward at that time. The Ward fired at and sunk a Jap midget sub on the entrance to Pearl Harbor before the Japanese planes attacked. The gun from the Ward is on display in St. Paul, Minnesota.

After shakedown training at Pearl Harbor, we were sent on to Enewitok. I would like to first mention one incident that happened during our shakedown at Pearl Harbor. We were having a ship to ship torpedo drill. When these drills are done, the destroyer firing the torpedo sets the depth setting on the torpedo to go under the target ship. The target ship follows the torpedo and rates the accuracy of the firing ship. One of the torpedoes that we fired had something wrong with its depth setting and after firing it, we heard loud unkindly words coming from the target ship. We had hit her in the propellers and even though those torpedoes did not have explosives, I am sure it gave the target ship quite a jolt. I guess we passed our test since we actually hit the target ship. I believe our skipper had to answer quite a few questions about that to the admiral in charge. We were ordered on to Enewitok to join a carrier task force. Traveling alone, I guess they were glad to see us leave Pearl.

One day on our way to Enewitok, we picked up an enemy aircraft. The closer it got we realized it was a big Mavis Japanese Bomber but not very fast. It was an excellent target. The Captain ordered us to use the newly developed anti-aircraft shells which were supposed to explode when they sensed metal. We loaded our forward five inch main battery and fired. The shells went out a short distance and then exploded, having sensed the metal of our own ship. Needless to say, the Jap Mavis flew on her way and reported our presence to Japan. Captain Outerbridge was so annoyed, he gave an order to take all those shells and store them away and never use them again. We probably unloaded them when we got to Enewitok and replaced them with our regular anti-aircraft ammunition. We had no more trouble the rest of the war.

We joined the third fleet for carrier attacks on Luzon. This was our first action in the Pacific. During this operation Twin Engine Bombers pass our ship out of our gun range but headed toward the fleet which was 20 miles from us. We were on what the Navy called "Birddog" duty. We immediately radioed our sightings back to the fleet. We waited and waited for word of their attack on the fleet but about ½ hour passed and the O'Brien was ordered back to the fleet and another destroyer sent to take our place. This was our first action in the Pacific and I believe the Admiral probably thought we were a new ship and not yet dependable.

As we were on our way back to the fleet, the Jap Bombers attacked the fleet from the rear. All Jap planes were destroyed and the O'Brien received a radio message congratulating our radar staff for our prompt reporting that saved many lives that day. I kind of laughed to myself after receiving this message because those Jap Bombers were low on the water in order to avoid our radar, but we saw them visually. All's well that ends well and the O'Brien's reputation was further established.

After the task force returned to Ulithi, the O'Brien was ordered to join the 7th fleet at Leyte in the Philippines. This fleet was under command of Admiral Kincaid but was jokingly called by many of us in the Navy as MacArthur's Navy. We quickly learned what the Navy men had been telling us about the Philippines. You are either the quick or the dead. I saw my first Jap suicide plane close-up while on deck in Leyte Gulf. He came in high to avoid our radar, cut his engine until he was about 5000 feet above us. He then revved his engine and came straight down at our ship, missing us by about 50 yards but I did get a good look at that big red ball.

CHAPTER 6

Captain Orders His Old Ship Sank

The next operation in which the O'Brien participated, her captain ordered his former command, another destroyer, sunk because of battle damage beyond repair.

It was in Ormoc Bay on December 7, 1944, that the O'Brien had her first experience with Jap suicide planes. As the troops started ashore, the Japs began swarming over the escorting destroyers and among the ships hit was the ill-fated USS Ward, the former command of the skipper of the O'Brien, Commander W.W. Outerbridge, USN, 3545 South Utah Street, South Arlington, Virginia. Aboard the Ward, Commander Outerbridge had the distinction of first engaging the Jap enemy on December 7, 1941, at Pearl Harbor – sinking a Jap sub while on routine patrol off the islands. Now, exactly three years later, the crew of the O'Brien valiantly fought fires on the Ward for more than an hour, finally had to abandon the ship and sink it by salvos from the O'Brien guns.

Lieutenant (junior grade) Robert F. Desel, USNR, of 158-18 Grand Central Parkway, Jamaica, Long Island, New York, assistant First Lieutenant of the O'Brien led the fire-fighting party aboard the Ward – which was in constant peril of the fire reaching the magazines. Ensign Lou Telbizoff, USNR, of 475 South Macomb Street, Monroe, Michigan, assistant engineering officer, was another O'Brien officer who distinguished himself in this battle to save the Ward.

During all of this rescue and fire-fighting action, the O'Brien was under almost constant air attack by Jap suicide dive bombers. Famed air ace, Major Richard Bong, USA, accounted for five Jap planes that day and you can be sure the men of the O'Brien were properly grateful for the air defense being given them, although their own anti-aircraft was almost ceaselessly barking into the sky.

One part of the Ormoc Bay operation that I have not seen written about was that right after landing our troops, we received a radio message that eight Japanese ships were coming down from the north to land Jap reinforcements where we had just invaded. The O'Brien was ordered to leave Ormoc Bay and intercept the enemy reported coming down from the north.

We started to head north when we received a radio message from the Marine Air Force base at Tacloban, Leyte telling us to return our ship, they would take care of the ships coming down from the north. Until we got that word, I felt it was almost suicide sending one destroyer against eight Jap ships. I was never so relieved after receiving the message from Tacloban, but as we returned to our ships at Ormoc Bay, Jap planes that were protecting the Jap ships coming down from the north, spotted us picking up our boats at Ormoc and began suicide attacks.

We fired at Jap suicide planes all afternoon and then returned to Leyte. When we anchored in Leyte Gulf, I received a wire that my first son was born and everything was okay. I guess Ellen, my wife, and I had a rough day on the same day because my son, Gary Michael Woods, weighted 9 lbs. 2 oz at birth.

Little did I imagine at that time that I would ever see him, but with the luck of the Irish, which was (DD725 O'Brien's call name) and my own prayers, I saw him grow up into a fine man. He was an officer in the Military Police in Korea and Vietnam. He has now retired as an Army Colonel and is nearly ready to retire from the Fort Wayne, Indiana police force as a Captain. He is now sixty-eight and I am eight-nine and we still play golf together, something I only dreamed of during World War II.

Photo # 80-G-335685   USS Ward burning in Ormoc Bay, 7 Dec 1944, with USS O'Brien fighting fires

SHIPS

(Time Magazine – January 7, 1945)

SENTRY'S DEATH

In the quiet, predawn hours of December 7, 1941, the USS Ward, a 23 year old, four piper destroyer, rolling back to Pearl Harbor from a routine patrol, picked up a startling report from a minesweeper: a mysterious object, possibly a submarine, had been detected in the darkness to the west. From the skipper's cabin, Lieutenant William W. Outerbridge, nervously proud of his first full command, hurried out to direct a search. Finding nothing, he gave the order to secure general quarters, went back to sleep.

But within two hours, he was again brusquely awakened. This time, lookouts could plainly see the shape of an unfamiliar (hence unfriendly) submarine conning tower in the murky dawn. At full speed ahead, Outerbridge pointed the Ward straight for the submarine. At 100 yards range, he ordered the No. 1 gun fire – The First U.S. Shot of World War II in the Pacific. The second shot struck the conning tower. Four depth charges finished off what turned out to have been a Japanese midget sub.

During the rest of the day, the 1,060 ton Ward, named after the first naval officer to be killed in the Civil War, remained on patrol. She ducked Jap air attacks, captured a motor-driven sam with three prisoners. From that day on, she was up to her gunwales in the Pacific War; she fought in the Solomons, bombarded Aitape, took part in the Aitape and Biak landings, and saw action at Cape Sansapor, Morotai, Dinagat, Leyte.

This month, her valiant career ended. The Navy announced that in supporting the landings at Ormoc, December 7, the converted destroyer-transport Ward, commanded by Lieutenant Richard F. Farwell, was stuck by aerial torpedoes along with the 1,450 ton destroyer Mahan, and had to be abandoned and sunk. They were the 48th and 49th U.S. destroyers lost in World War II. (The Ward was sunk by the USS O'Brien – Captain W.W. Outerbridge).

Then it was on to Leyte Island, and the O'Brien had her first taste of Japanese "kamikaze" suicide planes. In the early part of December 1944, Task Group 78.3, under the command of Rear Admiral Arthur D. Struble, was assigned to escort the U.S. Army's 77th Division to an amphibious landing at Ormoc Bay, Leyte. Twelve destroyers, including the O'Brien formed an elliptical screen around the task group. Besides the escort unit, the invasion fleet consisted of eight transports and 43 landing craft.

On December 6th, as Struble's fleet neared its objective, the sky turned cloudy and a ten-knot wind blew in from the northeast. Although several Japanese planes were sighted near the island, the enemy aircraft did not attack. The most annoying predicament that occurred during the approach to Ormoc Bay was the unexpected appearance of numerous small boats filled with curious natives. Each of the boats had to be stopped and searched by the escorting destroyers. The Laffey reported that the craft she investigated contained two Filipinos and a load of fish and vegetables.

At 0445, on December 7th, the O'Brien and Laffey were ordered to support minesweeping operations in the bay. The destroyers moved up astern of the minesweepers, about 2000 yards ahead of the assault force. Commander Outerbridge was directed to head for his attack station at 0600 and a half-hour later, the O'Brien opened fire on enemy barges, barracks and shore batteries. About 0700, the signal was given to cease firing and the order issued to "Land landing force." The O'Brien then swung along the northwestern shore of the bay, looking for other targets. She attacked and destroyed more barges, barracks, buildings and camouflaged artillery emplacements.

Suddenly, at 0800, several bogeys were picked up on radar and a minute later, a flight of Japanese two engine "Bettys" swarmed over the task group. A number of planes were shot down, but a few managed to weave their way through the heavy screen of anti-aircraft shrapnel. The USS Mahan and USS Ward quickly became unwilling victims to the fanatical kamikazes. One of the suicide planes crashed into the port side of the Ward, crushing fuel tanks as it plowed completely through the vessel. The unlucky destroyer-transport erupted in a ball of flames.

The O'Brien was ordered to stand by the Ward and render assistance. Commander Outerbridge dashed to the scene of the disaster at 27 knots. The O'Brien's skipper was very familiar with the burning ship. He was captain of the destroyer on December 7, 1941, when the Ward had the distinction of being the first American ship to engage a unit of the Japanese fleet - sinking a midget submarine off the entrance to Pearl Harbor, more than an hour before enemy planes appeared over the battleship anchorage. Now, exactly three years later, he was rushing to the aid of his former command. The O'Brien approached on the portside of the crippled vessel, but it was necessary to stand off 30 yards while fire hoses poured water into the burning hull.

William Outerbridge stated: "A fire-fighting party was not put aboard the Ward due to the danger of exploding ammunition magazines and the limited time available to fight the blaze. It soon became apparent that the flames could not be put out and the Task Group Commander ordered this ship to sink the Ward. The destroyer's aft magazine was hit by our shellfire and exploded. The ship sank within a matter of seconds."

Only six officers and 40 enlisted men survived the suicide plane's crash. Even while fighting fires and attempting to rescue men in the water, the O'Brien and other ships of the task group, were under constant attack by kamikazes. During the afternoon, two more destroyers, the USS Little and USS Lampson, were also clobbered by enemy aircraft.

After the battle, Commander Outerbridge formed a definite opinion on steps that should be taken for protection against this new form of Japanese assault: "When an alert is sounded and the plane is unidentified, the speed of individual destroyers should be increased to at least 15 knots. The ships should also be maneuvered on a zigzag course in order to confuse the aircraft in the early stages of contact. If the plane has been identified as enemy and appears to be attacking, the destroyer should be swung in such a manner as to have all six five inch guns firing at the aircraft. The target should be kept on the quarter, so that both aft 40mm mounts will bear on the kamikaze. When a ship opens fire, zigzagging should cease and speed increased to 25 knots until it is determined which vessel the plane is aiming for. During the aircraft's dive, the rudder should be put over and the ship turned in a circle while trying to evade the attack. If the kamikaze cannot be avoided, it is better to present a stern target than a bow target, because the damage sustained would probably be less vital to the destroyer's operation. Whereas, if it was hit in the bow, control of the ship and its guns would be lost and most of the key personnel either killed or wounded."

7 U. S. divisions, one from new Ormoc bay beachhead, close in for Jap kill on Le[...]

ALLIED HEADQUARTERS, Philippines, Dec. 8 (UP) — Seven American divisions, one of them lashing out from a new beachhead only three miles from Ormoc, churned the Japanese pocket in northwest Leyte from all sides today and complete liberation of the central Philippine island appeared to be in sight. "We will end it and we don't intend to take too long about it, either," Lieut. Gen. Walter Krueger, commander of the 6th army, told newsmen as the final offensive to crush the last 40,000 to 50,000 Japanese on Leyte got under way.

U. S. TROOPS were believed in Ormoc today after landing (A) 3 miles south of Japanese supply base on Leyte. Planes guarding new Task landing wiped out Nipponese convoy approaching Leyte from north (B). Japs landed 500 paratroops in the San Pablo area (C).

6000 Nippon troops killed in convoy bound for Leyte

ALLIED HEADQUARTERS, Philippines, Nov. 16 (UP). — American planes have wiped out an entire four-ship convoy with 6000 troops intended for Leyte and have sunk or damaged 14 other vessels in East Indies waters, it was announced today.

60 Yankees bomb Manila

Air Force Pool
The Japanese-controlled Manila radio said "about 60" American carrier-borne planes bombed Manila and Clark field today, the POC reported.

CHAPTER 7

The picture of my wife and newborn son was taken later on after we were hit at Okinawa by a Jap suicide plane and had returned to Mare Island, California for repair. I am the third from the left and fourth from the left was my bunkmate. When the ship was commissioned, we chose the first two bunks on the starboard side of the bow. He had the upper and I had the lower for the entire time on the O'Brien until the end of the war. His name was Lambright and he was from East Palestine, Ohio. After the war, we drove to East Palestine but could not locate him.

After every action, we felt our ship had made great strides in attaining the goal of maximum efficiency in battle. We are shipmates now, not just sailors; for each moment of mutual danger has added years to old friendships and we have come to love our ship, as one learns to love the things for which he fights. We know each other and know our ship and we love what we know. We are proud of our part in the fight.

There was no rest for the O'Brien after the savage action at Ormoc Bay. The battle-weary destroyer was assigned to Task Group 78.3 in preparation for the amphibious assault on Mindoro Island. In preparation for our next operation, the assault on Mindoro Island, Captain Outerbridge, for the first time, informed the entire crew about the Mindoro operation the day before we left Leyte. Unfortunately, it caused two of our men to take a rubber life raft, ammunition and food and go over the side together in the life raft around midnight as our invasion fleet slowly moved through the Surigao Strait (we called it the Suicide Strait), south of Leyte. these men were not missed until 8:00 a.m. the next morning while we were still underway to Mindoro. We worried that they would be captured by the Japs and forced to tell them where we were headed. We could picture the Japs waiting for us with suicide planes, etc.

Upon our return from Mindoro to Leyte, Captain Outerbridge was sent for by Admiral Kincaid. He was told that our two men were captured by Philippine guerrilla fighters and turned over to the Americans. They said they were survivors of the USS O'Brien, because the Mindoro operation was so dangerous they thought that the O'Brien would be sunk and they would be heroes. We never found out what happened to them. That was the last time the entire crew was told about an operation before we were in the middle of it.

About 0700 on December 15, 1944, the O'Brien was steaming on her fire support station – screening off the invasion beach. At 0710, orders were issued to land troops, and a few minutes later, the first soldiers waded ashore. But the Japanese were ready for the American fleet. Eight Zero fighters were sighted racing in low over the 2nd side of the beachhead. The task group opened up with a heavy barrage of gunfire. Six of the "Zekes" were ripped from the sky – two of them shot down by the hotshot gunners aboard the O'Brien. However, a couple of kamikazes evaded the exploding shells and crashed into LST's 738 and 472. Both landing craft were struck just forward of the superstructure and burse into flames. The O'Brien and other nearby destroyers, were immediately dispatched to the scene.

The O'Brien dashed from her screening station and pulled alongside LST 472. While attempting to put out fires on the landing craft, two men on the destroyer's forecastle were wounded when ready ammunition aboard the LST exploded. Fires on the stricken vessel continued to burn out of control and orders were soon given to abandon ship. Commander Outerbridge commented: "During this attack by the suicide planes, an excellent opportunity was afforded to observe enemy tactics. The aircraft flew in from the south – very low and just behind Ambolon Island. Because of land echo, their approach was not detected by radar. After the Japanese planes cleared the top of the island, they dropped down low over the water and fanned out to the northeast. All signs indicated that only a few of the aircraft were designated as kamikazes, while the others were acting as fighter escort. The suicide pilots closed the landing craft, but the escorts moved more to the east and eventually turned away. Immediately before we opened fire, the kamikazes commenced making "S" turns at high speed. Then they went into a steep climb, rising about 600 feet. From that altitude, they dove on their targets. This method of attach was used on LST's 738 and 472. In both cases, the aircraft rammed the ships from the leeward side."

At 1300 the O'Brien rejoined the task group. Moments later, more bogeys were reported. Fleet speed was increased to 20 knots and zigzag courses were ordered. About 1800, the O'Brien's radar picked up a bogey at 12 miles and coming in fast. Other enemy planes were reported by the USS Ingraham. At 1923, lookouts on the O'Brien sighted their target. After one salvo from the destroyer's sharp-eyed gunners, the kamikaze exploded. The next morning, more pips were spotted on the task force radar screens. During the afternoon, the weather worsened and all ships were warned that the CAP (Combat Air Patrol) would be flying low. For the rest of the day, most of the bogey reports turned out to be Americans. At 2100, a large formation of unidentified planes was reported 50 miles astern. A few tense minutes ticked by before the aircraft were announced to be friendly.

DADDY IS IN THE PHILIPPINES with the navy and you can imagine how happy he'll be to get this picture of his wife, Mrs. Raymond Woods of 51 R____ the st., and their seven-week-old son, Gary.

xxxxxxxxxxxxxxxxxxxxxxxxxxxxxx
Ray's First Picture of Gary
10 weeks old January 1945
xxxxxxxxxxxxxxxxxxxxxxxxxxxxx

xxxxxxxxxxxxxxxxxxxxxxxxxxxxxxxxxxxxxxxxxxxxxxxxxxxxxxxxxxxxxxxxxxxxxxxxxxxxxxxxxxxx
Ray (second from right)on a "Night on the Town" with his O'Brien buddies
vvvvvvvvvvvvvvvvvvvvvvvvvv----------------------------

Yanks strike deep ~~Mindoro~~
after 600-mile jump from Leyte

By WILLIAM B. DICKINSON

ALLIED HEADQUARTERS, Philippines, Dec. 16 (UP).—American invasion forces, pouring into at least three beachhe[...] after a 600-mile amphibious jump from Leyte to within 120 miles of Manila, struck deep inland on the western Philippines island [...] Mindoro today in a developing offensive threatening two of the island's main airfields. (The Japanese Domei Agency admitted [...] about one division—15,000 men—of American troops was debarking near San Jose, four[...] miles inland from the southwest coast of Mindoro and site of an airfield. The broadcast claimed that Japanese garrison units intercepted the invaders and said fighting "is now in progress.")

(A Japanese communique claimed that Japanese planes had sunk or damaged 2[...] American warships and transports in a series of attacks on [...] the Mindoro invasion armada Wednesday, Thursday and Friday. Listed as sunk were four transports, while eight [...]

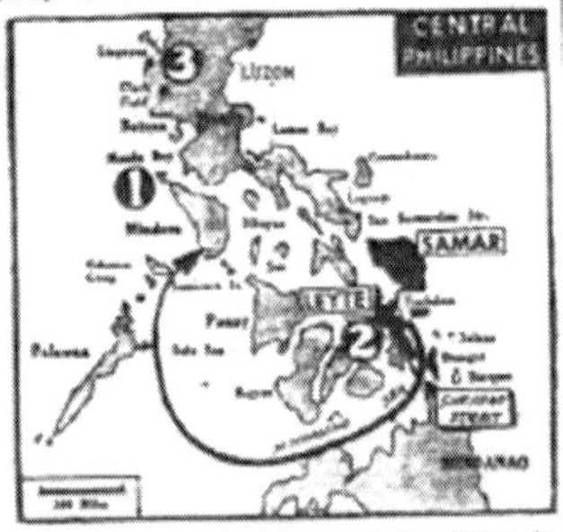

U. S. TROOPS were advancing from beachheads on Mindoro (1) today after a 600-mile amphibious jump from Leyte (2). Hundreds of American planes pounded Jap air bases in Luzon (3) to neutralize attacks on invasion convoy.

transports, two battleships, three cruisers and two cruisers or destroyers were "heavily damaged and set afire" and six unidentified vessels were "damaged.")

(Another Tokyo broadcast said a "violent" sea and air battle was in progress in the Sulu sea south of Mindoro.)

[Remaining column text largely illegible]

SITE OF AIRFIELD

Through intact landing sites were not disclosed, San Jose, four miles inland is the largest town in southwest Mindoro and the site of the biggest of two airfields in the area. A plantation railway links San Jose with two points on the coast, Caminawit Point and [...] a stagnation wharf.

Only scant opposition was reported in the first hours of the assault and American troops were described officially as slight, and landmarks warned that chances Japanese land, air and possibly naval reaction could be expected within possibly a matter of days. Mindoro is slightly less than 300 miles northwest of Leyte but Gen. Douglas MacArthur's communique announcing the landings said the invasion ships had traveled 600 miles west and north from Leyte bypassing Mindanao, Bohol, Cebu, Negros and Panay, all revealed to be largely in guerilla hands.

LUZON RIGHT MILES AWAY

Lemon, site of Manila and the main Japanese stronghold in the Philippines, lies only eight and a half miles across the Verde Island mega from the north coast of about. The Japanese were said to have plenty of troops [...]

[Right column text largely illegible]

INVASION RISKY

Lieut. Gen. Walter Krueger, commander of the 6th army, acknowledged that the invasion was risky but if successfully completed it virtually would seal the Japanese empire.

Gen. Douglas MacArthur reported in his communique that the invasion had cut the Philippines in two and "will enable us to dominate the sea routes which reach to the China coast."

"The conquests of Japan to the south are rapidly being isolated, destroying the legendary myth of the greater Asia co-prosperity sphere and imperiling the so-called Imperial phase." MacArthur said.

Mindoro's west coast lies along the south China sea opposite French Indo China. Both the China coast and the Japanese-within island of Formosa, are only 750 miles from Mindoro within easy range of American Flying Fortresses and Liberators. If based there, Fighter from Mindoro could range over virtually the entire Philippines archipelago.

MacArthur also disclosed that Filipino guerrillas operating under his command have seized large areas including strongly held coastal points and airfields on seven other islands in the central and southern Philippines among them Mindanao, Negros and Cebu.

AIRFIELD NEUTRALIZED

Carrier-based planes from a Pacific fleet task force teamed with MacArthur's land-based gunners and fighters in a mighty two-day air bombardment Thursday and Friday that virtually neutralized six enemy airfields in the Philippines in preparation for it's invasion of Mindoro. MacArthur reported that at least 204 Japanese planes were destroyed in combat and on the ground. Admiral Chester W. Nimitz announced at Pearl Harbor that his carrier planes alone had destroyed 174 aircraft, and it was not clear immediately whether these were included in the total announced by MacArthur.

The Japanese managed, despite, to set some troops into reinforced fighting fields. [...]

53

HEADED FOR ENEMY on the run. U. S. infantrymen race down ramps from LCI beached on Mindoro island as they forge onward in battle to oust Japs from Philippines. Yanks have met little resistance so far.—(Int.)

WASHINGTON, Dec. 16 (UP).—The invasion of Mindoro in the western Philippines was regarded here today as the most hazardous but potentially most profitable undertaking by American armed forces since the Pacific war began. Military observers believed that success of the Mindoro operation is the key to eventual reconquest of Luzon and the control of the strategically vital Philippines. The Philippines are absolutely necessary for the long-term plan to invade the Japanese homeland itself.

The landings are of such great significance and so fraught with possibilities that the Japanese may be forced to commit the remnants of their fleet to another battle with the U. S. Navy. No doubt the U. S. Pacific fleet commanders are alert to this possibility.

The fact that Gen. Douglas MacArthur has dared embark on the Mindoro venture even while engaged in a tough fight on Leyte is accepted here as an indication that his military forces are in a strong position as regards reserves.

The Mindoro operation should give the American command these advantages:

1. Force the Japanese to draw reinforcements from Luzon, and thus either weaken their garrison there or require them to send replacements from Formosa or the homeland.

2. Provide an ideal jumping-off base for an invasion of Luzon.

3. Facilitate ground-based air cover for the anticipated future landings on Luzon.

But no one here expects the Mindoro operation to be a pushover. By jumping clear over to the western side of the Philippines, MacArthur has taken a big gamble. The stakes are high but the potential gain is tremendous.

FLANKED BY JAPS

No matter how MacArthur routes his supply and communication lines to back up his forces in Mindoro, they will be flanked by Japanese-occupied islands. If they run from Leyte through the Visayan sea the lines must pass by Cebu, Negros, Panay, Masbate and a host of smaller islands where the Japanese undoubtedly have airstrips. If they run from bases in the south Pacific through the Sulu sea, then they must pass the Sulu archipelago, Mindanao, Palawan and many other lesser islands.

To protect these supply and communication lines MacArthur will have to gain and hold complete air domination over virtually all of the Philippines. The Navy already has given him a good start in that direction by its destructive carrier strikes on Luzon. In two days, Wednesday and Thursday, naval airmen destroyed 224 Japanese planes and bombed and strafed 90 more on the ground.

New U. S. fleet off Mindoro; Japs wait invasion of Luzon

By WILLIAM B. DICKINSON

ALLIED HEADQUARTERS, Philippines, Dec. 18 (UP).—The liberation of the Philippines gained momentum today with American forces driving 12 miles inland on newly-invaded Mindoro within 130 miles of Manila and splitting the Yamashita line on Leyte into three disorganized segments in a powerful offensive.

(Radio Tokyo said an American fleet of "considerable strength" had been sighted in the Sulu Sea south of Mindoro and speculated that another amphibious landing was in prospect, perhaps on Luzon, site of Manila and Gen. Douglas MacArthur's ultimate objective in the Philippines.)

REPAIR AIRFIELDS

American and Australian engineers on Mindoro, already were rushing repairs to capture San Jose airfield and building new air strips on what Gen. MacArthur called "excellent sites" to cover the next phase of the Philippines campaign.

Japanese resistance, both in the air and on the ground, continued negligible. Apparently paralyzed by the day and night raids on their Philippines airdromes by the American carrier and land-based planes, the Japanese were able to get few aircraft off the ground and most of them were shot down.

American patrol planes strafed and set afire a coastal vessel and two small freighters off the northeast coast, and damaged a third freighter off the east coast, but there was no official indication whether these were engaged in reinforcing the Mindoro garrison.

EXTEND BEACHHEADS

On Mindoro, invasion forces under Brig. Gen. William C. Dunckel, former member of MacArthur's planning staff, drove six to seven miles beyond the captured sugar town and airfield site of San Jose, five miles inland from the southwest coast, and extended the beachhead perimeter in either direction along the shore itself.

No Japanese remained in the southern part of the island, an official spokesman said, though a sizeable force was believed across the roadless mountains to the north. MacArthur said the American hold on southern Mindoro now could be considered "secure."

On Leyte, some 300 miles south-

east of Mindoro, Americans forces brought the final annihilation of 20,000 to 25,000 Japanese trapped

U. S. ENGINEERS today were rapidly preparing San Jose airfields (1) on Mindoro for clearance plane assaults upon Manila.

in the northwest corner of the island within sight with a series of surprise attacks from the south and east.

The 77th division swung west of the battleline above Cagua, a mile and a half north of Ormoc, and advanced seven miles in a wide flanking movement to within two miles from Valencia, headquarters of Lieut. Gen. Sosaki Suzuki, commander of the 35th Japanese army, and his staff.

Leyte's San Jose, two miles southwest of Valencia, and Tipio, a mile and a half south, were believed to have been captured in the advance.

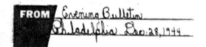

FROM Evening Bulletin
Philadelphia Dec. 28, 1944

USS O'Brien Newsletter

It is traditional in the Navy that the first deck log of the New Year shall be written in verse… This task fell to Lieutenant (jg) Robert Desel of Long Island, New York, and his very humble efforts are given space here for your pleasure:

> In the Philippine Islands, San Pedro Bay,
> In Eight fathoms of water the O'Brien lay.
>
> With 35 fathoms of chain on deck,
> The starboard anchor keeps us in check.
>
> Berth 52 is our spot,
> Let's hope the Japs don't make it hot.
>
> We are ready as we can be,
> The watch is at Condition Three.
>
> Darken ship and Condition Baker,
> Is set from Bow to after Perpendicular.
>
> On the line is Boiler Deuce,
> For auxiliary purposes it is in use.
>
> And now the watch is nearly over,
> The whole crew is disgustingly sober.
>
> While in the States the reverse is true,
> They are just starting, not nearly through.
>
> And we hope that soon we will be,
> There to join them on their next spree.

March 1945

CHAPTER 8

After the successful Mindoro operation, the O'Brien was ordered back to Leyte. Another task force was forming for the upcoming invasion of Luzon, the main island of the Philippines. On the night of January 2, 1945, the O'Brien rendezvoused with the bombardment ships of Task Group 77. The fleet was composed of two sections. The bombardment and fire support unit consisted of six battleships, six cruisers and 19 destroyers. The second unit included 12 escort carriers, 14 destroyers and six destroyer-escorts. Troop transports and landing craft were to follow two days later.

In the early hours of January 3, the battleship force slipped silently through the calm waters of the Surigao Strait, joining up with the carriers in the Mindanao Sea. Both sections then headed across the South China Sea. The weather was good and visibility excellent. There was no hiding from Japanese aircraft as suicide planes harassed the task group on the journey north. On January 4th, a kamikaze slammed into the USS Ommaney Bay. Fires burned out of control. Efforts to save the escort carrier were unsuccessful. The ship was abandoned and sunk by torpedoes.

The following afternoon, lookouts aboard the O'Brien spotted two "Zekes" racing in low over the water on a collision course. The lead plane maneuvered wildly through a hail of shellfire – finally veering off and splashing between the O'Brien and the HMAS Arunta. The second aircraft aimed straight for the Arunta, but tumbled into the sea, barely missing the stern of the Australian destroyer.

Before dawn on January 6th, Task Group 77 approached Lingayen Gulf on the west coast of Luzon. The battleships headed for their bombardment stations, while the carrier group remained in the South China Sea to provide air cover. By 0930, the bombardment vessels were in position. The escorting destroyers were stationed ahead and astern of the battle line. Orders were issued to commence firing and booming 16 inch shells began crashing into Japanese shore defenses.

At 1119, a Zero was sighted at 12,000 yards. The plane was flying at top speed, low along the edge of the beach. After a few salvos from the O'Brien's main battery, the aircraft swung out of range, but was still visible coming around astern of the fleet. The O'Brien dropped back, changing course as necessary while keeping all guns trained on the plane. When the "Zeke" again came within range, the O'Brien opened fire. The enemy pilot turned seaward, only this time, was greeted by U.S. Navy carrier fighters. Throughout the morning, Japanese aircraft nipped at the heels of the task group. At 1206, the USS Sumner reported she had been hit by a suicide plane. A minute later, the USS New Mexico was struck and at 1235, the USS Walke was smashed by a kamikaze.

U. S. jabs off Luzon have Japs punchy

By MAC R. JOHNSON

PEARL HARBOR, Jan. 8 (UP) —Tokyo reported today that one of four powerful American invasion armadas converging on Luzon in the Philippines has carried an unparalleled bombardment of beach defenses in the Lingayen gulf north of Manila into its third day and said a landing appeared imminent.

Some 400 to 450 American vessels are bound for "some not too clearly definable point on or near Luzon," Tokyo said, but warned that the American maneuvers were so complicated that false conclusions might be drawn.

YANKS SHELL COAST

Japanese broadcasts said American battleships and other warships, escorting 70 to 80 landing craft, penetrated Lingayen gulf to within a few thousand yards of the coast and were hurling shells into a 27-mile stretch between San Fernando and Damortis the latter about 116 miles north of Manila.

Fighters, bombers and dive-bombers from 16 aircraft carriers supported the bombardment with tree-top strafing and bombing attacks, Tokyo said.

"This is the enemy's usual tactics preceding a landing," a Japanese Domei dispatch from Luzon said. "Our men . . . are straining their ears for the sound of landing craft, for the enemy may approach the shores at any time."

U. S. CHIEFS SILENT

American headquarters here and in the Philippines remained silent on the enemy reports of impending landings, but announced new neutralization raids against Luzon and the capture of Palaun in the northeast corner of Mindoro island and 90 miles southwest of Manila.

The expanding American hold on Mindoro, coupled with the occupation of Marinduque, to the east, and Japanese reports of operations in Lingayen gulf, appeared to be setting the stage for an amphibious pincers assault against Manila.

Landings on Luzon both north and south of Manila would follow the Japanese pattern for the conquest of the island in December, 1941. The Japanese put their main force 66,000 troops ashore in the Lingayen gulf and soon afterward landed other sizable forces south of the capital which fell Jan. 2, 1942.

Planes of the 3d fleet, shifting their sights from bases in Formosa and Okinawa, farther north, joined with Gen. Douglas MacArthur's land-based aircraft on Saturday in destroying 45 Japanese planes and damaging 14 others in a series of raids in southern Luzon.

REPORT OTHER CONVOYS

In addition to the invasion armada already bombarding near Tokyo said three others sailing through Philippine waters apparently bound from Leyte to the Lingayen gulf.

PHILIPPINES

JAPS CLAIMED today U. S. naval ships were shelling Lingayen gulf from Bataan and San Fernando in Sac (1 in inset map). Tokyo also claimed great U. S. convoys pushing up from Mindoro and Leyte.

SPOT WHERE AMERICANS LANDED ON LUZON

LOW-LYING SHORELINE OF LUZON island around Lingayen gulf (above), made admirable landing place for American troops from 800 ship invasion armada who established 15-mile beachhead without loss of a man. Naval and air bombardment so reduced Jap defenses that "they refused to fight," one report stated. Troops are now less than 100 miles from Manila to the southeast.—(International)

Costly battle due on Luzon

By REUEL S. MOORE

WASHINGTON, Jan. 10 (UP). — Military observers today hailed the invasion of Luzon as a great step in the American drive toward Tokyo but warned that the island's strategic importance to Japan's defense system indicated a long and costly battle ahead.

Japanese strength on Luzon was estimated variously at from 200,000 to 280,000 men with a large part probably centered in the Lingayen gulf area where the initial American landings were made.

Experts here pointed out that Luzon not only is the heart of the Philippine economy, but the nerve center of Japan's defense system for the island. The enemy has had three years to bolster the island's fortifications and may well have chosen Luzon as the site for the do-or-die battle for all the Philippines.

WOULD WEDGE EMPIRE

American capture of the island would drive a strong wedge into the supply lines between Japan and her conquered southern empire in Malaya and the East Indies. And it would make the big inland-base of Formosa, north of Luzon, subject to steady aerial attacks.

LOGICAL ROUTES

The Japanese also opened their invasion of the Philippines with landings in the Lingayen gulf, with additional ones in Batangas and Tayabal provinces on the south. These are the logical routes to Manila, since the passage through Manila bay is guarded by Corregidor and its satellite forts.

Manila lies a little over 100 miles south of Lingayen gulf, and the terrain in between consists of much open country and good roads factors favorable to the use of mechanized equipment. The western approach would be more attractive from the standpoint of air power since the United States already has bases in Mindoro, just south of Luzon.

Mad Nippons hand-grenade Yankee ships

An NBC broadcast from Luzon said Japanese troops "gone mad" swam out into Lingayen gulf last night and threw hand grenades at Amer-

BRAINS OF U. S. NAVY AT LUZON

SOFTENING OF JAP defenses on Luzon and landing of Gen. Douglas MacArthur's land forces in successful invasion of Luzon was carried out by Navy according to plans of these experts led by Vice Adm. Thomas G. Kinkaid. On bridge of Kinkaid's flagship are (l. to r.) Vice Adm. Jesse B. Oldendorf, heavy bombardment commander; Admiral Kinkaid, Rear Adm. T. E. Chandler, commander cruiser division; Rear Adm. Russell S. Berkey, commander covering group, and Commodore V. H. Schaeffer, chief-of-staff.—(International)

60

Lingayen needs new capitol after Navy bombardment

JAP FORTIFICATIONS set up in capitol building at Lingayen made it necessary for U. S. Navy to train big guns on it, with results which are noted by American soldiers as they pass by.—(International)

Luzon invasion going better than expected

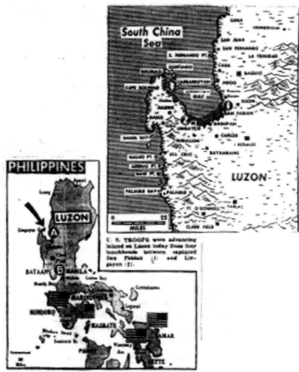

About 1315, Commander Overbridge was directed to cover a group of minesweepers as they swept a channel across the gulf. Then, at 1428, the O'Brien's luck ran out. A Zero suddenly dropped out of a low cloud formation. The kamikaze pilot flung his plane into a steep dive, brushing through the thick sheet of shrapnel thrown up by the destroyer. Seconds seemed like minutes as the O'Brien tried to evade the human bomb. But there was not enough time, one second short. The kamikaze clipped the O'Brien's stern – glanced off the port depth charge rack, then tumbled drunkenly over the side, slicing two holes in the destroyer's hull at the waterline. The aft crew compartment flooded and the ship listed five degrees to port.

Commander Outerbridge requested air cover and withdrew from the gulf for emergency repairs. Damage control parties immediately went to work. Mattresses and odd size pieces of lumber were jammed into the jagged holes and braced by shoring. Water was pumped out of the vessel, and the O'Brien dashed back to her station in the task group screen.

The following two days were a nightmare for the crew of the O'Brien. Mattresses and wood planks could not hold back the determined sea. But despite her wounds, the destroyer managed to keep up with the fleet. She chased off suicide planes, supported underwater demolition teams and blasted enemy shore installations. At 0700, on D-Day, January 9th, the invasion bombardment began. The O'Brien was assigned to a fire support unit which included the USS West Virginia, HMAS Shropshire and the Laffey. The group pounded landing areas off San Fabian. Cease firing was called at 0925 and the amphibious vessels headed toward the beach. The first four waves landed without opposition. The O'Brien provided call fire as directed from the Shore Fire Control. At 1300, the task group was attacked by suicide planes. Within a few minutes, the Shropshire was struck by a Zero. Another "Zeke" was spotted racing in low, about three miles from the O'Brien. The crippled destroyer opened up with every gun she had and the kamikaze splashed into the sea near the West Virginia.

After the beachhead was secured, the O'Brien steamed back to Leyte. Commander Outerbridge recorded his opinions concerning the Lingayen Gulf operation: "The kamikazes are skillful and determined. They will crash into a ship unless the plane Is either shot down, the pilot killed or wounded, or a radical movement on the part of the target throws off his aim. Believing that surface torpedo attacks by our destroyers will become less likely as the war progresses, and recognizing the need for greater anti-aircraft protection in the face of increasing numbers of suicide attacks, it is recommended that the aft torpedo tubes be replaced with a 40mm quadruple installation. Although 40mm guns will not stop a kamikaze in a steep dive, in other types of attack, these weapons might kill the pilot or cripple the plane to such an extent as to cause it to miss the target."

We had no one lost or wounded on his hit, but the largest crew quarters were completely flooded. We returned to Leyte for temporary repairs but they were unable to repair the O'Brien. We were sent to Manus Navel Base in New Guinea.

While in New Guinea, many of our experienced crew members were transferred to other ships or sent back to the States to train other crews. One of the fellows transferred back to the States was Lonas (Lonnie) Frey, Jr., a member of my VFW Post in Ottawa, Ohio now, and a retired crop duster pilot. We didn't meet until we lived in Ohio over twenty years. We did attend one of the early O'Brien reunions held in St. Louis, Missouri. Our executive officer Robinson, the officer who escaped with me uninjured when our Radar Room was hit by German Guns at Cherbourg, France, was transferred and received his own command.

Incidentally, we did have some entertainment while being repaired at Manus. We had an all male show put on by Irving Berlin; so much for any other good news during our three weeks near the equator.

After two weeks in dry-dock, the O'Brien was sufficiently repaired to join a fast carrier group for the first surface ship raid on Tokyo. The O'Brien sneaked to within 90 miles of the Japanese capital while on picket duty in advance of the fleet. Then about the middle of February, she was assigned to a fire support mission off Iwo Jima.

CHAPTER 9

On February 10, 1944, we were underway with Task Force 58.4 operating very fast carrier strikes against Tokyo, Iwo Jima and the Bonan Islands. A second attack on Japan was called off due to a typhoon with wild, heavy seas. It was almost impossible to maintain our fleet positions especially for the destroyer screen. Radar men had to be on our toes that night to avoid collisions. We were on standby at Iwo Jima and saw just one suicide plane try to hit a troop ship that was unloading near us. Fortunately, the Jap plane missed and crashed into the sea.

On March 21st, the O'Brien was attached to Task Force 54 as a fire-support ship for the invasion of Kerama Retto, about 25 miles southwest of Okinawa. The O'Brien was assigned to a bombardment group that included the Arkansas and the cruisers USS San Francisco and USS Minneapolis. At 0315, on March 26th, the O'Brien, along with the destroyers Laffey and Twiggs, formed an anti-submarine screen ahead of the bombardment column. Throughout the day, reports of enemy aircraft kept all ships at General Quarters.

The following morning, the O'Brien once again became a target for suicide planes. Commander Outerbridge described the action: "After operating in the screen off Kerama Retto, the O'Brien was ordered to report to Fire Support Unit Three at Okinawa. At 0618, suicide planes were reported in the area and all hands manned battle stations. Five minutes later, one aircraft from a loose group of eleven overhead was observed to be diving on this ship. We had identified about eight of the planes as friendly F4F's and TBF's.

"The O'Brien maneuvered radically with hard right rudder and all 20mm and 40mm batteries that could bear opened fire on the onrushing aircraft. The kamikaze was hit many times. It burst into flames at 300 yards and splashed about 75 yards on the starboard beam. Another suicide plane was immediately sighted heading straight down and aiming for the O'Brien. We swung hard left, attempting to bring the forward five inch battery to bear, while all other guns fired continuously at the diving aircraft. The plane was peppered with shrapnel, but managed to level off moments before it struck the O'Brien. The kamikaze crashed through the port side of the superstructure. As it tore through the starboard side, a 500-pound bomb broke loose from the plane and exploded on the weather deck. Fires instantly blazed topside."

Ellman Hodge was in the galley just forward of the explosion. He was thrown violently against the bulkhead and severely injured. Despite his wounds, Hodge was able to grab a fire hose and pour water on the flames. Commander Outerbridge reduced his ship's speed to ten knots and swung into the wind to facilitate fighting the raging fires. The USS Shannon and USS Gwin quickly arrived to offer assistance. However, since enemy planes were still in the vicinity, it was decided that neither vessel should come along-side. The Shannon and Gwin remained nearby, screening the crippled destroyer.

By 0650, all fires were under control and the O'Brien headed for the Kerama Retto transport anchorage. The wounded personnel were transferred to the USS Drew. The Gwin searched the attack area for any crew members who might have been blown into the sea. Casualties aboard the O'Brien were heavy, 28 men killed, 76 injured, and 22 missing.

The Captain again, as he did after Cherbourg, looked into the destroyed CIC (Radar Room) and gave everyone who survived in that room an advancement in rating. I now was the Radar man 2/c that I should have gotten months earlier but lost because of my overindulgence on fifteen cent rum cokes at our stop at Balboa, Panama Canal Zone.

In his report of the disaster, Commander Outerbridge stated: "The importance of immediate and conclusive identification of every plane in sight cannot be overemphasized. Recognition of several planes in a group is not sufficient. Each individual aircraft must be identified. During this action, the importance of the 40mm battery was clearly dramatized. In a surprise attack, these mounts can be brought to bear easier and faster than five inch guns."

Following temporary repairs at Ulithi, the O'Brien set out on her long voyage home across the Pacific. In only nine months of active duty, the O'Brien earned six battle stars. There were not many U.S. Navy destroyers that could boast that record. Lieutenant P.O. Vail, Jr., USN, whose mother, Mrs. Rhetta Vail resides at 611 West Thomas Street, Hammond, Louisiana, Executive Officer, although badly burned, remained at his post throughout the fight to save the ship.

In talking to some of the men with general quarter stations on the after part of the ship, they jumped into the water when the Jap suicide plane hit the bridge. They said while in the water, they watched the O'Brien completely inflamed and smoking as it moved away. They said they were sure she would sink, but as you know, she did not sink and after controlling the fire, the O'Brien picked up the men in the water. All our radiomen in the room next to our Radar Room or CIC (Combat Information Center) as the Navy called it, were killed; all the men in our Radar Room were wounded. I was sent aboard the USS Drew, acting as a hospital ship at Kerama Retto, checked out and returned to the O'Brien the next day.

Two horrible sights we will never forget while wounded and sitting on the fore castle, wrapped in blankets. We looked up to see two men's bodies hanging over the yardarm of the mast, held there by their blood soaked uniforms. The other was the sight of a crew member so badly burned that his entire back began to fall off and was pushed back. One other day I shall never forget was observing the burial at sea of 28 of our dead.

I was very lucky my burns were not serious. I looked worse than I was, my hair was burned, my arms and face were black. I did have one scar on my face that took a couple of months to fade away. The only comical thing I can think of at this time was, as we were transferred to the hospital ship, our names were being checked off by Lt. Baldwin, who worked with me in our radar room. As I approached him, I waved and started to pass onto the hospital ship. He stopped me and asked, "Who are you?" When I got on the hospital ship, I saw myself in a full mirror and realized why he didn't know me.

The O'Brien Lies at Anchorage in the Keramas. South Shore Line of Aka Shima in Center Background, Mar. 29, 1945.

CONFIDENTIAL   DECK LOG—REMARKS SHEET   *OKINAWA*   PAGE 86

O'BRIEN (DD725)   MONDAY   20   MARCH   19 45

0-4
Steaming on base course 095 T, 095 PGC, 105 PSC at speed 11 knots, in company with TF 54. OTC is CTF 54 in USS TENNESSEE. Screen Commander is Commander Destroyer Squadron 60 in USS BARTON. Formation 5RD. O'BRIEN in station #18 of circular screen, bearing 225 T, distance 10,000 yards from guide (USS IDAHO), guide bearing 2,000 from fleet center. Material condition Baker and condition of readiness III set, ship darkened. Boilers 2 and 3 in use for all purposes. 0045 c/s to 13 knots, commenced zigzagging in accordance with plan #6, USF 10A. 0126 Ceased zigzagging, resumed base course. c/s to 11 knots. 0132 c/c to 049 T, 046 PGC, 050 PSC. 0206 c/s to 10 knots. 0230 Commenced steering various courses and speeds and proceeded to sortie with TG consisting of USS ARKANSAS, SAN FRANCISCO, MINNEAPOLIS, LAFFEY and TRIGGS. 0315 Task Group formed up to eastward, heavy ships in column, Destroyers formed A/S screen #53, O'BRIEN taking station #1. Steadied on base course 045 T, 044 PGC, 048 PSC at speed 10 knots. 0335 c/c to 315 T, 314 PGC, 318 PSC. 0350 c/c to 045 T, 044 PGC, 048 PSC.

Lt. (jg) USNR.

4-8
Steaming as before on base course 045 T, 044 PGC, 048 PSC, speed 10 knots. 0415 c/c to 135 T, 134 PGC, 132 PSC. 0428 c/c to 180 T, 179 PGC, 184 PSC. 0437 c/c to 225 T, 224 PGC, 222 PSC. 0442 c/c to 045 T, 044 PGC, 048 PSC. 0500 c/c to 000 T, 359 PGC, 003 PSC. 0514 c/c to 270 T, 269 PGC, 268 PSC. 0545 Proceeding on various courses and speeds to station K-17. 0615 All hands to General Quarters, steamy planes in area. 0727 Secured from General Quarters, steamy planes ahead of area. Set condition of readiness III, set material condition Baker. 0730 On station K-17 commenced patrolling station on courses 240 T and 060 T, speed 12 knots.

Lt. (jg) USNR.

8-12
Steaming on courses 060 T and 240 T at speed 12 knots patrolling station K-17. 1110 c/s to 15 knots. 1155 Inspected magazines and s.p. samples. All conditions normal.

Ensign, USNR.

12-16
Steaming as before on various courses and speeds patrolling station K-17. 1234 Unidentified aircraft bearing 265 T, distance 36 miles. 12A0 General Quarters for air alert. 1247 Unidentified aircraft identified as friendly. 1309 Secured from General Quarters, set condition III.

Lieutenant, USNR.

16-18
Steaming as before on various courses at various speeds patrolling station K-17 at speed 15 knots. 1731 General Quarters for air raid alert. Enemy planes in area.

Boatswain, USNR.

18-20
Steaming as before on various courses and speeds, patrolling station K-17 at speed 15 knots. 18A0 Proceeded on various courses and speeds to take night station in area P-3. Darkened ship. 1916 Secured from General Quarters, set condition of readiness III and material condition Baker. 194O On station in area P-3 commenced patrolling station on northerly and southerly courses (011 T; 010 PGC, 008 PSC and 191 T, 190 PGC, 193 PSC) at speed 15 knots.

Lt. (jg) USNR.

20-24
Steaming as before on courses 011 T, 010 PGC, 008 PSC and 191 T, 190 PGC, 193 PSC patrolling 30 degrees either side of course at speed 15 knots.

Lt. (jg) USNR.

71

CONFIDENTIAL   PAGE 87

DECK LOG—REMARKS SHEET

UNITED STATES SHIP   O'BRIEN (DD725)   Tuesday 27 March 45

0-4 Steaming on various courses at 15 knots, patrolling picket station P-3 off Kerrama Rhett. Steaming on boilers #2 and #3 for all purposes. Ship darkened. Condition III watch set, material condition Baker set. 0155 General Quarters for air raid alert. 0230 Secured from General Quarters, set condition watch III and material condition Baker. 0350 Changed base speed to 10 knots.

J. W. _____, Ensign, USN.

4-8 Steaming as before in patrol area P-3 off Kerama Rhette, steering various courses and speeds to conform to patrol area. 0403 Secured from General Quarters, no unidentified aircraft in the vicinity, set condition III watch, material condition Baker. 0545 Detached by CTG 51.1 and ordered to report to CTF 52 in accordance with instructions in CTF 52 Operation plan 2-45. Proceeding on various courses and speeds to rendezvous with Fire Support Group #3 in Fire Support Area #5 off Chinawa Island. 0618 General Quarters for air alert. 0623 Sighted enemy fighter plane diving on the ship; opened fire with all available guns. Plane burst into flame and crashed about 100 yards on the starboard beam. 0624 Another enemy fighter seen diving on the ship. Maneuvered radically attempting to bring forward battery to bear, opened fire with all available guns. 0624.5 Enemy plane crashed into superstructure amidships, port side, tearing through superstructure to starboard side. Following damage caused: Main Radio completely demolished, CIC wrecked and all equipment either badly damaged or destroyed, all radars destroyed, both sound stacks damaged and gear inoperative. Starboard 40mm twin demolished, port 40mm twin damaged and inoperative. One forward 20mm destroyed. Starboard torpedo director damaged and inoperative. Number one fireroom out of commission due to completely demolished intakes and damage to steam and feed water piping. Number two boiler completely flooded. Forced draft blowers 1 and 4 badly burned. All electrical circuits and equipment demolished from amidships passage to wardroom and upward from main deck. General area frame 65 to 100 both sides, main deck starboard side dished in one foot and ripped along, seam frames 75 to 95. Spaces demolished:- wardroom, pantry, galley, provision issue room, torpedo work shop, log room, sick bay, laundry, uptake space forward fire room, starboard side of sound hut and CIC Radar transmitter room, forward 40mm ready service room, radio central. Forward stack damaged beyond repair. Superstructure deck ripped up from Frame 65 to 100. Starboard side 40mm gun deck blown up 20ft. Salt, fresh water and high pressure air lines in damaged area beyond repair. Starboard side after bulkhead forward fireroom warped, bulkheads to #1 and 3 lower rooms warped in vicinity of main deck. The following personnel casualties were sustained. Officer killed in action:

Brown, Wilbert Collins 334334, Lt (jg) USN; Enlisted men killed in action: Malunas, Anthony Joseph 847 24 94 SM1c, V6, USNR; Byrge, Daryl ___ 77 77 SoM3c V6, USN, SV; Deese, William Carl 263 72 66 S1c V6, USNR; De Freho, Wilbert Clarke 249 90 27 S1c, V6, USNR; Duncan, Johnnie Earl 892 76 30 S1c V6, USNR, SV; Fairbrook, Warren Sealye, 377 06 33, MTlc (T) V6, USNR; George, Thomas William 942 41 60 F1c, V6, USNR, SV; Linn, John Alexander 655 00 01 RM2c (T) V3, USNR; Mason, Elvin Ray 659 74 50 FN2c, V6, USNR; Miller, Robert Curtis 826 20 14 S2c SV, USN; Mooneyham, Charles Edward 566 02 33 S1c, V6, USNR; Mosley, John Clayton 831 22 10 S1c V6, USNR, SV; Murphy, Clyde Monroe Jr., 892 75 75 S1c, V6, USNR, SV; Morris, Vernon Logan 275 29 83 S2c, V6, USNR; Passerelli, John Anthony 908 17 07 S1c, V6, USNR, SV; Petersen, Tiggs Verne 886 15 52, TM3c, V6, USNR, SV; Pfeiffer, Paul Andrew 223 57 76 CTM (AA) USN; Purple, Orville Richard 895 00 44 S1c, V6, USNR; Ramsey, Glenn Raymond 638 02 50 RM1c (T) V3, USNR; Sowell, John Samuel 892 76 15 S1c, V6, USNR, SV; Sauble, Anthony William J 21 51 36 TM1c, USN; Spencer, William Ross 969 17 06 S1c, V6, USNR, SV; Steadl, William Jennings Bryant, Jr., 358 01 51 S1c, USN; White, Arnold (n) 234 35 69, RM3c, USN; Winter, August Henrich 328 35 66 CTM (AA) USN. Men missing as result of action: Angelopoulos, George (n) 642 50 45 S1c V6, USNR; Brightwell, Fred Ross 347 04 58 Cox, USN; PCM17, Fletcher Patrick Jr., 265 70 05 CSM (T) USN; Clsowski, William Frank 808 07 06 S1c, V6, USNR, SV; Collins, Daniel Raymond 820 27 92 S1c, V6S; Cook, Hugh Oliver 892 83 45 SF2c (T) V6S; De Salvatore, Rudolph Joseph 803 80 51 S1c V6S; Dickson, Austin (n) 892 75 92 S1c, V6S; Diehl, Leon Alfred 244 86 84 RM2c (T) V6, USNR; Dilger, Robert Harry 299 88 00 CMT (AA) USN; Hagan, Bob Fortune 382 04 61 CFMM (AA) USN; Hartwell, Francis Paul 378 07 66 RM3c (T) V6, USNR; Higgins, Virgil 290 68 34 CBM (PA) USN; Jordan, Lemuel Joseph 643 28 37 FN2c V6S; Kellogg, Kingdon Albert 822 40 89 GM3c (T) V6S; LeBarr, Norman Floyd 403 03 58 ML1c V6, USNR; Merchant, John Gayle 887 30 13 S1c V6S; Rolfe, Richard Howard 238 81 03 TM3c, USN; Rowin, George Joseph 944 07 82 S1c V6S; Sellers, John David 892 76 05 S1c V6S, USNR; Thorpe, Earl Ernest 617 91 10 S1c, V6S, USNR; Mitchell, William Watts 657 44 99 GM2c (T) V6, USNR; Officers wounded in action: Vail, Powell Prestridge 100178 Lieutenant, USN; Outerbridge, William Woodward 61472 Commander, USN; Houck, Leroy Price 227139 Lt (jg) USNR; Glaswell, William Erasmus 226683 Lt (jg) USNR; Brewster, Robert Charles 126377 Lt (jg) USNR; Elliott, Edward Warburger 389559 Ensign USN; Telkhnoff, Louis Everett 361668 Ensign, USNR; Cederlof, George Marvin 4XC495 Boatswain, USN; Enlisted men wounded in action: Boney, Wilbert Samuel 656 30 79 GM3c V6, USNR; Brooks, Roland, Vaughan 607 27 32 SC1c V6, USNR; Butcher, Arthur 828 66 84 S1c, V6, USNR; Cameron, William Dottie 403 70 99 CRM (AA) (T) USN; Celand, Pete Marion 821 93 84 FN2c V6S, USNR; Church, William Stanton 612 33 30 GM2c, V6, USNR; Cole, Anderson Nelson 949 17 74 S1c, V6S, USNR; Cook, Carl Leo 856 14 79 MM3c V6S, USNR; Creighton, William Peter 603 14 30 F1c, V6, USNR; Davis, Jever Delbert 931 25 70 S1c, V6S, USNR; Deary, John Joseph 616 65 65 RdM3c (T) V6, USNR; Emery, Thomas Duane 615 74 64 MM3c V6, USNR; Engebretson, Arthur Barnard 703 87 85 SM3c V6, USNR; Faulkner, Orval Dean 321 57 39 EM1c USN; Forgione, Carmen Andrew 741 91 39 S1c V6, USNR; Mallan, Edward Campbell 892 76 23 S1c V6, USNR; Hayde, Eugene Joseph 409 75 17 CMT (AA) (T) V6, USNR; Hill, James George 234 45 01 S1c, USN; Ho ____ 6LC 95 12 FN1c, V6, USNR; King, Do ____, Robert Raymond 300 25 26 MT1c USN; Johnston, Mason Eugene ____ len 317 10 79 F3c, V6, USNR; Lemieux, Ernest Stanis Tol 91 20 S1c Tb, USNR; MacDonald, ____ William 202 43 93 MM2c, USN; Sargent, Jacob Roger

72

CONFIDENTIAL   PAGE **88**

DECK LOG—ADDITIONAL REMARKS SHEET

UNITED STATES SHIP   O'BRIEN (DD725)   Tuesday 27 March 45

ADDITIONAL REMARKS

4-8 (Continued) 321 20 06 BM1c USN; Smith, Arvel Elroy 932 72 35 F2c, V6S, USNR; Sullivan, Donald Ryence, Jr., 815 75 43 S1c, V6S, USNR; Velotto, Frank Louis 809 73 00 S1c, V6S, USNR; Weiss, William Clarence, Sr., 943 61 23 S1c V6S, USNR; Edwards, Willey Thomas 656 86 27 S1c V6, USNR; Harris, James William 666 54 03 TM2c V6, USNR; Good, John Bruton, 790 54 14 CWT (AA) (T) V6, USNR; MacArthur, William Everett 833 96 96 S1c, V6S, USNR; Baum, Roy Edward, 282 97 33 SC1c USN; Bevan, Robert Davenport SoM1c 710 17 82 V6, USNR; Conklin, Charles Timothy 711 79 52 RdM3c V6, USNR; Hodge, Elman Woodrow CK3c 647 74 96 V6, USNR; Hughes, Charles Jennings Bryan, Jr., V1c V6S, USNR; Hundley, Eugene Keith QM3c 576 27 55 V6, USNR; Kelley, Paul Wilson F1c 965 86 55 V6S, USNR; McLamb, Gaston Charles F1c 833 94 98 V6S, USNR; O'Hara, Francis Gerard S1c 712 44 21 V6, USNR; Reid, David Cochrane S1c 892 75 99 V6S, USNR; Schafman, Sydney (n) QM3c 826 42 36 V6S, USNR; Truitt, Griffin Ezra S2c, 934 29 74 V6S, USNR; Weinzierl, Joseph William, Jr., S1c 896 42 73 V6S, USNR; Woods, Raymond Paul RdM3c 202 22 V6S, USNR; Adams, Billy Burton SK1c 359 98 66, USN; Baker, Aloysius, Michael MoMM2c 629 46 95 V6, USNR; Barrenco, Salvatore, John S1c 626 57 86 V6, USNR; Carpenter, Burley William WT3c 931 34 60 V6S, USNR; Carroll, John William 12c, 606 23 50, V6, USNR; Chaisson, John Henry SF2c (T) 203 35 50 V6, USNR; Cypher, Philip Robert F1c, 40 89 35 V6, USNR; Corvin, Luther Warren S2c, 969 17 32 V6S, USNR; Davis, George Gilbert S2c 969 17 86 V6S, USNR; Denny, Everette Gabriel S1c 892 61 93 V6S, USNR; Ellis, Forrest Sean F1c 892 44 03 V6S, USNR; Hanson, Donald Thomas GM3c 345 72 57 USN; Houdek, William Peter S1c 815 08 77 V6S, USNR; Kreiss, William George F2c 221 00 38 USN; Leddon, Robert Eugene SoM3c 842 85 73 V6S, USNR; Lankowski, Chester Joseph CM3c 300 66 77 USN; McKay, Robert Ralph S1c 825 34 27 V6, USNR; Melton, Everett Alton TM3c 665 61 75 USN; Nix, Roy Brinson S1c 938 98 42 V6S, USNR; Schweitzer, Edward Lawrence F1c 936 62 98 V6S, USNR; Vassalotti, Robert Anthony S1c 742 32 44, V6, USNR; Verna, Louis Joseph S1c 256 57 59 USN; Walk, Robert Orville MT2c 450 24 93 V6, USNR; 0650 Fires under control, steering various courses and speeds, returning to transport area.

         H. L. KUEHN,
         Lieutenant, USNR.

8-12 Steaming as before proceeding to transport area. 0845 Came alongside starboard side of LCS DREN (AP482) and transferred following wounded: Officers - Vail, Powell Prestridge 100178 Lieutenant, USN; Glassell, William Erasmus 226880 Lt. (jg) USNR; Brewster, Robert Charles 256577 Lt. (jg) USNR; Elliott, Edward Marburger 309539 Ensign, USN; Tabinsaff, Louis Everett 383696 Ensign USNR, Enlisted men - Baum, Roy Edward 282 97 33 SC1c USN; Bevan, Robert Davenport SoM1c 710 17 82 V6, USNR; Conklin, Charles Timothy RdM3c 711 79 52 V6, USNR; Hodge, Elman Woodrow CK3c 647 74 96 V6, USNR; Hughes, Charles Jennings Bryan, Jr., V1c V6S, USNR; Hundley, Eugene Keith QM3c 576 27 55 V6, USNR; Kelley, Paul Wilson F1c 965 86 55 V6S, USNR; McLamb, Gaston Charles F1c 833 94 98 V6S, USNR; O'Hara, Francis Gerard S1c 712 44 21 V6, USNR; Reid, David Cochrane S1c 892 75 99 V6S, USNR; Schafman, Sidney QM3c 826 42 36 V6S, USNR; Truitt, Griffin Ezra S2c 934 29 74 V6S, USNR; Weinzierl, Joseph William, Jr., S1c 896 42 73 V6S, USNR; Woods, Raymond Paul S1c RdM3c 202 22 V6S, USNR; Denny, Albert Samuel 656 30 79 GM3c V6, USNR; Brooks, Roland Vaughan 600 27 32 S1c V6, USNR; Butcher, Arthur 828 66 84 S1c V6, USNR; Cameron, William Dutkie LD3c 70 99 CM3c (AA) (T) USN; Celani, Pete Marion 821 93 84 RM3c V6S, USNR; Church, William Stanton 612 53 30 GM3c V6, USNR; Cole, Andrew Nelson 969 17 31 S1c V6S, USNR; Cook, Carl Lee 856 14 79 EM3c V6S, USNR; Creighton, William Peter F43 14 30 F1c V6, USNR; Davis, Dewar Delbert 931 25 70 S1c V6S, USNR; Deery, John Joseph 818 65 65 RdM3c (T) V6, USNR; Emory, Thomas Duane 615 73 64 S4M3c V6, USNR; Ingebretsen, Arthur Barnard 703 67 85 SM3c V6, USNR; Faulkner, Orval Dean 321 57 29 Bkr1c USN; Fargiano, Carmen Andrew 761 91 39 S1c V6, USNR; Hallen, Edward Campbell 892 76 23 S1c, V6S, USNR; Hayda, Eugene Joseph 409 75 17 CWT (AA) (T) V6, USNR; Hill, James George 234 45 01 S1c, USN; Howard, Robert Raymond 300 25 24 WT1c, USN; Johnston, Nessen Eugene 640 95 12 Ph1c V6, USNR; King, Donald Allen 117 10 79 S1c, V6, USNR; Lemieux, Ernest Stanie 761 91 20 S1c V6, USNR; MacDonald, Clarence William 202 43 90 QM3c, USN; Margent, Jacob Roger 321 20 06 BM1c, USN; Smith, Arvel Elroy 932 72 35 F2c, V6S, USNR; Sullivan, Donald Ryence, Jr., 815 75 43 S1c, V6S, USNR; Velotto, Frank Louis 809 73 00 S1c, V6S, USNR; Edwards, Willey Thomas 656 86 27 S1c V6, USNR; Harris, James William 666 54 03 TM2c V6, USNR; Good, John Bruton 790 54 14 CWT (AA) (T) V6, USNR; MacArthur, William Everett 833 96 96 S1c, V6S, USNR. 1022 Transfer completed. Cleared side and lay to in transport area awaiting orders.

         H. L. KUEHN,
         Lieutenant, USNR.

12-16 Lying to as before in Transport area.

         D. F. NEAL,
         Lt. (jg) USNR.

16-20 Steaming as before off transport area at Kerama Rhetto on various courses and speeds. 1645 Held burial services at sea for the following men killed in action: Officer - Brown, Albert Cullen J34354 Lt. (jg) USN, Enlisted men - Bielunas, Anthony Joseph 647 24 94 S1c F6, USN; Byrge, Darryl 828 29 77 SoM2c V6S, USNR; Sease, William Carl 263 72 66 S1c V6, USN; De Fr. Albert Clarke 249 90 27 S1c V6, USN; Duncan, Johnnie Earl 692 76 30 S1c V6, USN; Fairs, Warren Seslye 377 06 33 SF1c (T) V6, USN; George, Thomas William 943 41 60 F1c V6, USN; Linn, John Alexander 655 00 04 RM3c (T) V5, USNR; Meaux, Elvin Ray 659 74 90 BM3c V6, USNR; Miller, Robert Curtis MoMM S1c 14 GM3c V6S, USN; Anonymous, Charles Edward 504 02 53 S1c, V6S, USN; Lesley, John Clayton 651 22 10 F1c V6S, USNR; Murphy, Clyde Morris Jr., R43 14 94 S1c

         T. A.

| DECK LOG—ADDITIONAL REMARKS SHEET | CONFIDENTIAL |

UNITED STATES SHIP _____ O'BRIEN (DD725) _____ Tuesday 27 March 45

ADDITIONAL REMARKS

16-2v (Continued) V6S, USNR; Norris, Vernon Logan 275 29 83 SFc V6, USNR; Passarelli, John Anthony 408 17 07 S1c, Vb3, USNR; Peterson, Viggo Verne 886 15 52 TM3c V6S, USNR; Pfeiffer, Paul Andrew 323 57 74 CTL (AA) USS; Purple, Orville Richard 895 00 44 S1c V6S, USNR; Ramsey, Glenn Raymond 638 02 90 S1c (T) V], USNR; Sowell, John Samuel 892 74 15 S1c V6S, USNR; Snoble, Anthony William 321 51 34 TM1c USN; Spencer, William Ross 949 17 04 S1c, S61, USNR; Wandt, William Jennings Bryant Jr., 358 01 51 S1c USN; White, Arnold 234 35 69 RM3c USN; Winter, August Henrich, 328 35 69 CEM (AA) USN. Three unidentified bodies were also buried. 1708 Completed burial services. 1810 Proceeding to join CTG 51.1 in night retirement. 1830 Ordered to take station 1,000 yards astern of rear transport on base course, 180 T, 179 PGC, 192 PSC, speed 12 knots. 1842 arrived on station.

Lieutenant, USNR.

20-24
Steaming as before on base course 180 T, 179 PGC, 192 PSC at speed 12 knots. 2015 Commenced zigzagging. 2150 Ceased zig-zagging, steadied on base course 180 T, 2200 c/c to 210 T, 209 PGC, 216 PSC. 2210 Commenced zig-zagging as before. 2345 c/s to 8 knots. 2350 Ceased zig-zagging, resumed base course 210 T, 209 PGC, 216 PSC.

V. T. KOGLER,
Lt. (jg) USN.

CONFIDENTIAL

DECK LOG—REMARKS SHEET

PAGE 90

UNITED STATES SHIP O'BRIEN (DD725)

Wednesday 28 MARCH 1945

0-4 Steaming on base course 210 T, 209 PGC, 211 PSC at speed 8 knots in company with TG 51.1. OTC is CTG 51.1 in USS MOUNT McKINLEY. Steaming on #4 boiler for all purposes. Ship darkened. Condition of readiness III set, material condition Baker set. 0008 c/c to 225 T, 224 PGC, 222 PSC. 0050 c/s to 10 knots. 0053 c/c to 345 T, 344 PGC, 338 PSC. 0065 c/s to 15 knots. 0040 c/c to 305 T, 304 PGC, 304 PSC. 0045 c/c to 335 T, 4 PGC, 354 PSC. 0105 c/c to 025 T, 024 PGC, 027 PSC. 0121 c/c to 070 T, 069 PGC, 4 PSC. c/s to 8 knots. 0200 c/c to 035 T, 034 PGC, 038 PSC. 0223 c/c to 065 T, 014 PGC, 018 PSC. 0252 c/c to 000 T, 359 PGC, 356 PSC. 0244 c/s to 12 knots. 0316 Lighted fires under #3 boiler. 0330 c/c to 030 T, 029 PGC, 032 PSC. 0331 c/c to 000 T, 359 PGC, 356 PSC. 0357 Cut in #3 boiler on main line.

K. F. _____
Lt. (jg) USNR.

4-8 Steaming as before on various courses at various speeds maintaining station 1,000 yards astern of last transport in right hand column of formation at speed 12 knots. 0550 Entered transport area off Kerama Rhetto. 0557 Held General Quarters for dawn alert. 0610 Flash blue, control green. 0620 Flash red, control green. 0638 Flash blue, control green. 0723 Secured from General Quarters, set condition III watch, material condition Baker. 0730 Proceeding alongside USS DREW to deliver mail. 0740 Passed mail to USS DREW. 0747 Completed passing mail and proceeded to steer various courses at various speeds in transport area.

C. W. _____
Boatswain, USN

8-12 Patrolling as before on various courses at various speeds in transport area. 1030 Lying to astern of AK 240 taking on stores from boat. 1040 Proceeding to APA 162. 1120 Lying to on port quarter of APA 162 in transport area, awaiting return of ambulatory patients from APA 162 to O'BRIEN by boat.

W. _____
Ensign, USN.

12-16 Steaming as before on various courses and speeds in transport area off Kerama Rhetto. The following officers and men returned to the O'BRIEN from APA 162: Officers - Vail, Powell Prestridge 100178 Lieutenant, USN; Glassell, William Erasmus 230883 Lt. (jg) USNR; Brewster, Robert Charles 254377 Lt. (jg) USNR. Enlisted men - Bass, Roy Edward 282 97 33 SC1c, USN; Bevan, Robert Davenport 710 17 62 SoM1c V6, USNR; Conklin, Charles Timothy 711 79 52 RdM3c V6, USNR; Hodge, Elmus Woodrow 647 74 96 CK3c V6, USNR; Hughes, Charles Jennings Bryan, Jr. 833 97 06 F1c V6S, USNR; Hundley, Eugene Keith 576 27 53 GM3c V6, USNR; Kelley, Paul Wilson 965 86 55 F1c V6S, USNR; McLamb, Caston Charles 833 96 98 F1c V6S, USNR; O'Hare, Francis Gerard 712 44 24 S1c V6, USNR; Reid, David Cochrane 992 75 99 S1c, V6S, USNR; Schafner, Sydney 826 42 36 GM3c V6S, USNR; Truitt, Griffin Ezra 934 29 76 S2c V6S, USNR; Weinsierl, Joseph William, Jr. 896 42 73 S1c V6, USNR; Woods, Raymond Paul 808 02 29 S1c V6S, USNR. 1550 Stationed anchor detail, proceeding to anchorage in Kerama Rhetto anchorage.

H. L. _____
Lieutenant, USN.

16-20 Steaming as before on various courses and speeds to anchorage. 1605 Anchored in Kerama Kaikyo anchorage in 17 fathoms of water with 60 fathoms of chain out to port anchor on following true bearings: Right tangent 012; Left tangent 027; Left tangent on nearest rock 340 and rock 118. 1834 Underway on various courses and speeds proceeding to another anchorage. 1758 anchored in 24 fathoms of water with 60 fathoms of chain out to port anchor off No. J1 shoal on the following true bearings: Rock 325; Right tangent 030; Left tangent 338; Rock 148; Left rock 037; Peak 273. Various units of U.S. fleet present. 1839 Darkened ship. General Quarters for dusk alert.

J. V. _____
Lt. (jg) USN.

20-24 Anchored as before, ship at General Quarters. 2014 Secured from General Quarters, set condition III watch, material condition Baker.

G. W. _____
Boatswain, USN

75

"List of officers and enlisted men who have performed outstanding actions with home address, description of action and awards granted."
Reference —- ALPAC #278

Silver Star
W.W. Outerbridge, Comdr., USN., 61472, 3545 South Utah St., Fairlington, South Arlington, Virginia.
Award of Silver was made for service during the invasion of Normandy and the Bombardment of Cherbourg. (Copy of actual citation is not available, having been destroyed in subsequent battle damage.)

Bronze Star
K.G. Robinson, Lt. Comdr., USN., 81320, 55 East 86th St., New York, New York
Next of Kin: Mrs. Elizabeth L. Robinson (wife)
"For meritorious service in support of sustained operations against the enemy and for conspicuous service, gallantry, acts of heroism in actual combat with the enemy, and in the Baie de la Seine and during the bombardment of the Cherbourg area, Lieutenant Commander Robinson conducted himself in outstanding manner and in accordance with the highest traditions of the United States Naval service, carrying out his duties as executive officer, navigator, and Combat Information Officer in such a manner as to reflect great credit on himself and the Navel Service."

P.P. Vail, Lieut., USN., 100178, 611 W. Thomas St., Hammond, Louisiana
Next of Kin: Mrs. Rhetta Miller Vail (mother)
"For distinguishing himself by heroic and meritorious conduct in sustained operations against the enemy in the Ormoc Bay Area, Leyte, Philippine Islands. Lieutenant Vail directed the fire fighting operations of the USS O'BRIEN which was attempting to extinguish fires on the USS WARD in spite of the constant threat of enemy air attack and danger from exploding ammunition. His conduct throughout distinguished him among those performing duties of the same character."

Commendation Ribbon
J.W. Mackenzie, Lt. Comdr., USNR., 69723, 1373 Newport Ave., Northampton, Pennsylvania
Next of Kin: Mrs. Helen Eileen Mackenzie (wife)
"For outstanding performance of duty as Engineer Officer of the USS O'BRIEN during action with enemy shore batteries in the Cherbourg area of the coast of France. This vessel was struck by a major caliber shell which resulted in the destruction of electrical and radar circuits and the starting of electrical fires. Lieutenant Commander Mackenzie acted courageously, calmly, and

efficiently, and with his repair parties extinguished the fires and isolated the circuits involved. This action reflected great credit on his leadership and ability to organize and instruct men under his command. His conduct during this emergency was in accordance with the highest traditions of the Naval Service."

J.A. Groden, Lieut., USNR, 96529 Garfield Street, Cambridge, Massachusetts
Next of Kin: Miss Eleanor G. Groden (sister)

"For meritorious conspicuous service in support of sustained operations against enemy in the Baie de la Seine area and in the bombardment of Cherbourg area. Lieutenant Groden, as Gunnery Officer of the USS O'BRIEN, inflicted damage upon enemy shore installations while supporting Ranger troops of the United States in the Baie de la Seine and in harassing enemy large gun batteries in the Cherbourg area. Lieutenant Groden conducted himself in such a manner in carrying out his duties as Gunnery Officer as to reflect great credit upon himself and the Navel Service."

E.J. Dougherty, Lieut., USNR, 96589, 245 Rosemont St., La. Jalla, California
Next of Kin: Mrs. Grace R. Dougherty (wife)
"For conspicuous service and gallantry in combat with the enemy and heroism in action. During the bombardment of the Cherbourg area this vessel was struck by a major caliber shell resulting in considerable damage and loss of life. In carrying out his duties and First Lieutenant and Damage Control Officer, Lieut. Dougherty led his repair parties promptly and courageously to the scene of the damage and without regard to personal safety, immediately set about the task of confining the damage and giving aid to the wounded. Lieutenant Dougherty's unselfish devotion to duty and leadership reflects great credit upon himself and is in accordance with the best traditions of the Naval Service."

H.J. Crocker, Lieut. (jg), USNR, 113182, 14 Florence Street, Rockland, Maine
Next of Kin: Mrs. Flora H. Crocker (wife)
Awarded the Commendation Ribbon for service during the Invasion of Normandy and the Bombardment of Cherbourg. (Copy of the actual citation is not available, having been destroyed in subsequent battle damage.)

N.F. Taylor, Lieut. (jg), USNR, 185294, 213 Williamsboro Street, Oxford, North Carolina
Next of Kin: Mrs. Martha F. Taylor (mother)

"For conspicuous service, gallantry and heroism in combat with the enemy. When the USS O'BRIEN was struck by a major caliber shell near Combat Information Center area, which was his battle station, Lieutenant Taylor immediately, and without regard to his personal safety, proceeded to the scene of disaster and aided in controlling the fire and in succoring the wounded with great zeal and with the best traditions of Naval service."

William Cullen Brown, Lieut. (jg), USN, 334354, 273 Elmira Ave., Algiers, Louisiana
Killed in action 27 March 1945.
Next of Kin: Mrs. W.C. Brown
"For distinguishing himself by excellent service in support of landing operations against the enemy in the Ormoc Bay Area, Leyte Island, Philippine Islands, on 6-7 December, 1944. As Office in Charge of the Amidships Repair Party on the USS O'BRIEN, when she was ordered to proceed to the aid of the USS WARD, in an attempt to put out a fire, Lieutenant (jg) Brown directed the fire fighting parties under hazardous conditions. With complete disregard for his own safety, he immediately set about his task with all the equipment at this disposal. For his conduct throughout he is commended and authorized to wear the Commendation Ribbon."

Roy Christner Wetterhall, Lieut. (jg), (SC) USNR, 182724, 536 Walnut St, Ann Arbor, Michigan
Next of Kin: Mrs. Elwyn H. Wetterhall (mother)
"For meritorious and conspicuous service in combat with the enemy in the bombardment of the Cherbourg area. When this vessel was struck by an enemy shell, which resulted in considerable damage and in the death and wounding of several men, Lieutenant Wetterhall proceeded to the scene immediately and without regard to his own safety, assisted in combating the fire and in succoring the wounded, thereby preventing any further loss of life and damage to the ship. Lieutenant Wetterhall's courageous devotion to duty reflects great credit upon himself and is in accordance with the best traditions of the Naval service."

Robert Frederick Paul Desel, Lieutenant (jg), USNR, 256038, 158-18 Grand Central Parkway, Jamaica, Long Island, New York.
Awarded the Commendation Ribbon for service during the Invasion of Luzon (Lingayen Gulf), Philippine Islands, January, 1945. (Copy of the citation is not available, having been destroyed in subsequent battle damage.)

Bielunas, Anthony Joseph, Machinist's Mate First Class, USNR, New Jersey
Killed in action 27 March 1945.
"For distinguishing himself by excellent service in support of landing operations against the enemy in the Ormoc Bay Area, Leyte Island, Philippine Islands, on 6-7 December 1944. As a member of the Repair Party on the USS O'BRIEN, when she was ordered to put out a fire, Bielunas, with complete

disregard for the danger of exploding ammunition at the scene of the fire, manned one of the fire hoses and kept a continuous stream of water on the flames. For his conduct throughout he is commended and authorized to wear the Commendation Ribbon."

Burns, Edward Joseph, Carpenter's Mate Third Class, USNR, Peoria, Illinois "For distinguishing himself by excellent service in support of landing operations against the enemy in the Ormoc Bay Area, Leyte Island, Philippine Islands, on 6-7 December 1944. He was a member of the Repair Party on the USS O'BRIEN, when she was ordered to proceed to the aid of the USS WARD in an attempt to put out a fire. Burns, with complete disregard for the danger of exploding ammunition at the scene of the fire, manned one of the fire hoses and kept a continuous stream of water on the flames. For his conduct throughout he is commended and authorized to wear the Commendation Ribbon."

Faulkner, Orval Dean, Baker First Class, USN, Miami, Florida "For distinguishing himself by excellent service in support of landing operations against the enemy in the Ormoc Bay Area, Leyte Island, Philippine Islands, on 6-7 December 1944. As a member of the Repair Party on the USS O'BRIEN, when she was ordered to proceed to the aid of the USS WARD in an attempt to put out a fire, Faulkner, with complete disregard for the danger of exploding ammunition at the scene of the fire, manned one of the fire hoses and kept a continuous stream of water on the flames. For his conduct throughout he is commended and authorized to wear the Commendation Ribbon."

Shelley, Don "T", Seaman First Class, USNR, R 4 Loris, South Carolina "For distinguishing himself by excellent service in support of landing operations against the enemy in the Ormoc Bay Area, Leyte Island, Philippine Islands, on 6-7 December 1944. He was a member of the Repair Party on the USS O'BRIEN, when she was ordered to proceed to the aid of the USS WARD in an attempt to put out a fire. Shelley, with complete disregard for the danger of exploding ammunition at the scene of the fire, manned one of the fire hoses and kept a continuous stream of water on the flames. For his conduct throughout he is commended and authorized to wear the Commendation Ribbon."

The World Wide Question

When comest the hour all arms laid down
A battlefield rewakes a town;
Children step from 'neath their fear
From Mother's eye there drops a tear.

We ask thee Lord, is there a way
To bring the peace this very day?
Love back to souls, away this hate
The bone is deep; we're not too late?

Peaceful lands now realms of horror
Hued with red; these tools of war
Hast made all mankind blind with lust
Forgetting good and pure and just.

We give to you our prayers and thanks;
Full command! The place in ranks,
For only you can see this done;
Earth's peace restored and victory won.

Written after
the Battle of Cherbourg
by

Glen Raymond Ramsey, Radioman
Killed in Okinawa

They That Have Parted

We knew their laughs, their jobs, their faults;
It seems but yesterday,
They joined in battle, work and play.
Or, could it have been today?

They were a part, one of our team,
Their absence leaves a gap.
Can good replacements, such as they
Be found to meet the Jap?

We pray for those we've left behind;
May God's will be done!
They have paid the highest sacrifice;
The O'Brien salutes each one!

Written after
the Battle at Cherbourg
by

Glen Raymond Ramsey, Radioman
Killed at Okinawa

Escape hatch used by the author after being hit by the suicide plane at Okinawa.

Suicide Planes Get O'Brien After Ship Saw Heavy Action

With 296,000 man-hours of repair work already completed on her, the valiant destroyer USS O'Brien—a veteran of a dozen world-famed battle actions—is being put back into fighting trim at Mare Island Navy Yard and soon will be back in service with the Pacific Fleet, fighting in the showdown at the door step of Japan.

The story of the 15-month old ship, which has lived two lifetimes for an average craft in that time, was released yesterday and with it came the revelation that the O'Brien was on hand when the USS Ward, Mare Island record ship which fired the first shot in World War II, met her final fate on Dec. 7, 1944, three years after she opened hostilities.

(The Ward sank a Jap while on routine patrol outside Pearl Harbor some seven hours before the actual attack began.)

ACTION AT ORMOC BAY

... ... O'Brien .... at Ormoc Bay when the O'Brien had her first experience with Jap suicide planes which hit the Ward. The Mare Island ship—built in 17½ days during World War I—was the former command of the O'Brien skipper, Commander W. W. Outerbridge, South Arlington, Va. Outerbridge was aboard the Ward when war was declared.

The crew of the O'Brien valiantly fought fires on the Ward for more than an hour. Finally had to abandon the job and sink the Ward.

Lieutenant (jg) Robert F. Deal, USNR, Jamaica, Long Island, N. Y., assistant first lieutenant of the O'Brien, led the fire fighting party aboard the Ward — which was in constant peril as the fire reached the magazines. Ensign Lou Tribault, USNR, Monroe, Mich., assistant magazine officer, was another O'Brien officer who distinguished himself in this battle to save the Ward.

BAGS GOT 5 PLANES

During all of this rescue and fire-fighting action, the O'Brien was under intense combat air attack by Jap suicide dive bombers. Passed air arm, Major Richard Boyg, USN, accounted for five Jap planes that day and was ... ...

82

U.S.S. O'Brien, Hero Destroyer, Is Under Repair At Mare Island After Jap Attack

(Continued From Page 1) ed. February 25, 1944, at Boston navy yard, has been all over the world on her battle strikes—ranging from D-Day at Normandy, to Pacific landing on Okinawa on the very doorstep of Japan. Her combat assignments have carried the O'Brien on an express-train rampage from one battle action to the next—from just off the French coast to 90 miles from Tokyo — sometimes with a whole skin and sometimes "patched up" but still looking for trouble and dishing it out.

AT NORMANDY

First action for the O'Brien was shepherding a fleet of 50 large infantry landing ships into flaming, erupting "Omaha Beach" at Normandy on D-Day. This done, she poured it on to join a task group assigned to bombard Nazi coastal gun positions at Cherbourg.

On June 25, 1944, the O'Brien was well inshore, screening some minesweepers, and slamming away at the German batteries with her five-inchers. The famed only battlewagon USS Texas was standing further offshore, pumping her 16-inch projectiles into the Cherbourg area directly over the O'Brien. The little destroyer, however, was scoring so effectively on the Nazi gun positions that the Germans switched their attention to the O'Brien from the bellowing Texas. Once the powder-blackened snouts of the Nazis' long rifles were concentrated smack on the O'Brien it was just a matter of time until the weaving, dodging destroyer was straddled and one shell hit on the after part of the bridge. This occurred

about noon of the 25th and the O'Brien stayed on the job, although badly battered, hurling shells ashore until 3:30 p.m.

HIT BY BATTERY

The Texas also was hit by a shore battery and the O'Brien was ordered to make smoke to cover her. In spite of her grievous wounds, the gallant little ship layed a screen in front of the Texas, undoubtedly saving her from more hits from shore.

After temporary repairs in England, the O'Brien shoved off for the States and Boston navy yard for major repairs.

In August, 1944, in company with a new carrier, the O'Brien sailed south through the Panama Canal and headed for Pearl Harbor—from whence she joined the Third Fleet in carrier strikes against Luzon, in connection with the Leyte landing operations.

MINDORO INVASION

Following the Ward action on Dec. 15, 1944, the O'Brien participated in the invasion of Mindoro. This action was "very calm," according to the battle-wise O'Brien-ers.

Back to Leyte from Mindoro, the O'Brien was dispatched to join the pre-invasion bombardments of Lingayen Gulf. On January 5, 1945, the destroyer was gingerly threading its way around the gulf, escorting minesweepers and demolition teams in small boats. The next day, under terrific Jap suicide air attack, the O'Brien was hit by a "Zeke" (Jap single-engi(en) plane) in a suicide dive on her port side. The plane exploded, opening a large hole in the destroyer's side.

NOT THAT EASY

With mattresses and odd bits of lumber jammed in the gaping hole in her side, the O'Brien steamed back into the fray on the morning of January 7—and she stayed at her job until the troops arrived and took over on January 9, 1945, returning then to Leyte for temporary repairs.

Proceeding from Leyte to another advanced base for more complete repairs, the O'Brien managed to get back into the thick of things in less than two weeks—joining a carrier group for the first raid on Tokyo—and approaching within 50 miles of

the Jap capital while on picket duty far ahead of the rest of the fleet.

From that raid, the O'Brien made all available knots down to Iwo Jima with a fast carrier force to give that invasion air and ship fire support. After four days around Iwo Jima, the ever-busy destroyer ripped back up the line for another Tokyo strike—and had to fight through a tremendous typhoon to get there. This particular strike did not come off as the weather was too foul to permit planes to be launched.

ACTION OFF OKINAWA

On March 26, 1945, the O'Brien, still in the thick of things, was standing off strategic Kerama Retto Island, about 25 miles from Okinawa, where Army troops were about to force a landing. Suicide planes were again in evidence—but nothing happened to the O'Brien until the following morning, March 27, when, a little after 6 o'clock, a Jap suicide plane skimmed out of low clouds and, before the O'Brien gunners could fire, hit just aft of the bridge, exploding a magazine and spreading death and destruction throughout the ship.

Twenty-eight men were killed outright, 22 were missing and more than 100 were injured.

PRAISE FOR GALLANTRY

Although the whole crew conducted themselves in the best tradition of coolness under fire, Ellman Woodrow Hodge, CK 2/c, Negro officers' cook, goes the highest praise for his gallantry. In the galley just forward of the explosion, Hodge was thrown violently about his compartment and severely injured—but when the first officer reached the scene of the worst fires, Hodge was already playing a fire hose on it despite his own condition.

His mother, Mrs. Josephine A. Hodge, lives at P. O. Box 744, Charlotte Amalie, St. Thomas, Virgin Islands.

Lieutenant P. P. Vail Jr., USN, whose mother, Mrs. Rhetta Vail, resides at 411 West Thomas Hammond, Louisiana, exe officer, although badly remained at his post throughout the time to save the ship

83

CHAPTER 11

After returning to the O'Brien, we spent one night at Kerama Retto and I was assigned a 20mm anti-aircraft gun as my station. Thank God we weren't attacked that night, because it had been two years since I was given just verbal training on use and operation of the 20mm. I could picture myself shooting everything except the target. It was a long night. The next day, another destroyer was hit by a suicide plane in the afterpart of the ship and still had all its radar, radio and engines and was ordered to escort the O'Brien back to Pearl Harbor.

Another odd thing that happened, because we had taken Kerama Retto five days before Okinawa was invaded, April 1, 1945, we passed the Okinawa invasion fleet going into Okinawa as we're returning to Pearl Harbor. With one engine, no galley, no radio, radar or sonar, I was given the job of helmsman, steering the O'Brien back to Pearl Harbor. One night on the way back, I had the helm, waves were breaking over the bridge and I thought the barometer was going to break the bottom of the glass. We were running along the edge of a storm. I had trouble keeping the O'Brien on course, but with God's help, we made it to Pearl Harbor.

Another story I would like to tell is about our Captain and the Captain of the destroyer that led us back to Pearl Harbor. They were friends and a few days before reaching Pearl Harbor, the Captain of the other destroyer, sent a message to the O'Brien by signal light saying, "You have 90 days availability at Pearl Harbor Navy Yard." Our commander Outerbridge was so angry at getting this message he informed our crew over our PA system that he would see about this. He said we were entitled to return to the States for repair after our second and long stay in the Pacific. However, the captain of the other destroyer knew our commander's feelings about returning to the States and sent the message as a joke. A correcting message was sent shortly after the first one stating, "You have 90 days availability at Mare Island, California."

When the O'Brien pulled alongside the dock at Mare Island Navy Yard, a band was playing but our crew didn't realize it was for us and were not prepared. The ship was heavily damaged and the crew was in dungarees handling the lines. The news media took pictures of our damage and it made the West Coast papers the next day.

There were railroad representatives on the dock selling tickets home. I chose Western Pacific. It was a long, slow ride through the mountains which took three days in the old style coaches with straight up seats. I had a thirty day leave so I bought two tickets for the return trip with my wife. When we returned to Oakland, California, we were tired and dirty and couldn't wait to get on the bus to Vallejo. We sat in the bus terminal for about an hour waiting for a bus marked Valley Jo, not seeing any, we finally asked and were told they run every ten minutes; that was when we learned how to spell Vallejo, California, where Mare Island Navy Yard is located. Our living conditions at Mare Island were great. We were in newly built and furnished Quonset Hut apartments. Purchased our food from the commissary, which had many foods civilians couldn't buy because of shortages due to the war and rationing. Movies in beautiful theaters were ten cents. My wife and I had more fun there than at any other Navy Base.

After nearly 300,000 manhours, the O'Brien was ready for sea again. We were told we would be going down to San Diego on a shakedown run. That was fun depending on how you looked at it. Many of the wives got on a train for San Diego, including mine, when the O'Brien left Mare Island. Many other wives returned home. We left Mare Island and San Francisco late in the day. It was night by the time we reached the waters off the West Coast and headed south for San Diego. We found these waters to be quite rough. Operating our new radar, I was reporting contacts to the Captain on the bridge. He and his officers peered through the night with their glasses but could see nothing. The same contacts also appeared on their new bridge radar monitor. It was several hours before we realized that our radars were 180 degrees off. Meaning contacts ahead of us on the radar were actually behind us and vice versa.

When we arrived in San Diego and met our wives, the captain was, well, let's say unhappy because he didn't tell his wife we were headed for San Diego per naval orders and she had returned home. To add insult to injury, after a few days in San Diego, they could not repair the problem and we were ordered back to Mare Island. One of the men got off the ship and notified the wives. They took the train back to Mare Island, arriving before we did, and were inquiring when the O'Brien would get in. This added to the previous annoyance of the Captain.

This gave all lucky husbands and wives who stayed out there at least two more wonderful weeks. In order to keep the crew occupied, I was sent one day to operate the radar on a Navy Yacht, which they used to train new radar operators. While sailing in San Francisco Bay, a young officer called down to me from the desk above and wanted to know why I didn't report the contact above. I said I've been watching it and at its current course and speed, the ferry wouldn't come within 500 yards of us. I was not required to do that job again. After all I had been through for nearly two years operating radar in both the Atlantic and the Pacific, in all kinds of weather and battle conditions, I could not get excited about a ferry boat.

The day finally came when we were to leave Mare Island again, this time for the forward area. I can't say I was anxious to leave after having one radar room blown up by German guns at Cherbourg and having my ship hit twice by Jap suicide planes, one of which destroyed my radar room again and earned me the Purple Heart. Would the third time be the charm? I was finally one of the last men to board ship as my wife remained on the dock. The thoughts running through my mind were, would I ever see my wife and my first son, who was less than a year old, again?

CHAPTER 12

We laid in San Francisco Bay overnight with the Indianapolis and assumed we would leave with her the next day for Pearl Harbor, nut when we looked for her the next morning, she was gone. Upon arriving at Pearl Harbor, we inquired about her and they told us she left two days ago. This surprised us because we made our trip from San Francisco to Pearl Harbor in good time. In a couple of days, we had the news of the first atomic bomb dropped on Hiroshima. This was such wonderful news because it could mean the end of the war. The Navy interviewed me and several other sailors on the O'Brien as to our feelings. It was a difficult interview after all we'd been through. I still have a copy of that radio tape.

Then the bad news came about the sinking of the Indianapolis with over 600 lives lost. She was sunk after delivering that first atomic bomb. We felt sick for them and their families, but now we knew why the Indianapolis had made such a high speed run from San Francisco and Pearl Harbor to the forward base. She had delivered the first atomic bomb.

After our normal shakedown at Pearl Harbor, we left for the forward areas and heard a second atomic bomb had been dropped on Nagasaki and the Japanese had agreed to unconditionally surrender. Navy ships throughout the Pacific were given assignments as the Battleship Missouri entered Tokyo Bay for the signing of the peace. The assignment for the O'Brien was to patrol Osaka, Japan with another British destroyer while the peace was being signed in Tokyo Bay. The only incident that happened there was that we spotted a floating mine but after firing at it and hitting it many times, we decided it was just a net buoy that had broken away. Of course, that night lying in my bunk, listening to the water just outside my head, a thought came to me and kept me awake most of that night: "What if we did get hit by a mine now after the war was over and all dangers were to cease?"

In a few days, we were ordered into Tokyo Bay due to the approach of a typhoon. We entered Tokyo Bay and dropped anchor among other ships. The wind was blowing very hard when I decided to go up on deck from my crew's quarters. The hatch I came out of onto the main deck was up forward of the ship. As I opened the hatch, I saw the stern of two destroyers moving toward me and our ship. I looked down at the water to see if we were underw2ay, but we weren't. The storm had ripped the two destroyers from its moorings and they were being blown toward the O'Brien. I watched one destroyer brush down the side of the O'Brien, completely wrecking our motor whale boat on the port side. I did not see any other major damages but the Navy ordered the O'Brien into Yokosuka Naval Base for further examination, especially our propellers.

Being one of the first American ships to dock at a Japanese Navy Yard, we got to see Japanese prisoners cleaning up the area near where we docked. The biggest surprise we got was when the crew was allowed several hours of liberty, which enabled us to examine areas in the Naval Base. We saw a classroom with a mockup of a two man Japanese sub, complete machine shops cut into the cliffs overlooking Tokyo Bay, an abandoned 14 inch gun emplacement with Jap uniforms thrown on the floor of the huge gun mount. We saw a warehouse with about 50 small 12' speed boats with large inboard engines and hollow hulls. I figured the Japanese plan was to load the hull of each of these speed boats with high explosives and crash them into our ships on entering Tokyo Bay. At this high speed and small size, they would be difficult to hit or avoid especially at night.

We were nervous, but about four of us proceeded into a nearby town. One incident had me concerned for a moment when a Japanese man walked directly toward me and raised his hand and pointed to the cigarette pack I had in my blouse pocket. With a sigh of relief, I handed him the pack of cigarettes. He turned and walked away. We also walked up a hill with houses and several Japanese girls on the porch of one of the houses tried to talk to us. We were able to do this because we had been given Japanese=-American dictionaries. By pointing to words in these dictionaries, we were able to carry on minor conversation. After awhile, the girls came out with a bottle of Saki and small cups. They offered us a drink. We were careful and watched them pour all the cups and they drank from theirs. It was very good rice wine and we enjoyed it. After thanking the girls, we let them know we were due to go back to the town and onto our ship. They said we will walk with you. They did, but walked behind us all the way to town, where we waved as we left them. Where we had expected to see hate, we saw nothing but friendship, much to our pleasant surprise.

We left Japan with other ships and picked up men throughout the Pacific who were eligible for discharge. Three of these ships, including the O'Brien, returned many of these men to San Diego. Just before leaving Japan, I developed a painful pianidal cyst due to sitting for hours on steel chairs while on radar watch until we got back to the States. I chose to try to ride it out but one night at sea, the pain was so bad I had to wake the ship's doctor. He lanced the cyst and relieved the pain, but I was sent to Balboa Naval Hospital as soon as we reached San Diego. I was operated on and spent three weeks in the hospital recovering. Then I was given several weeks leave to go home and see my wife and son, Gary, who was now nearly a year old and walking. He was a beautiful, little boy with curly blond hair. I had to leave Ellen and

Gary again and return to the hospital in San Diego. After two short check ups, I was given orders to fly commercial airline to New York and Lido Beach for my discharge. That was a lucky break, because most men were sent back for discharge by train.

William Woodward Outerbridge
Rear Admiral, U. S. Navy, Deceased

Admiral Outerbridge was born, April 14, 1906, in the British Crown Colony of Hong Kong. His father was a British sea captain – his mother had been a U.\ S. Army Nurse in the Philippines. At the age of six, he went to Dover, England to school. When his father died a year later, his mother returned to Middleport, Ohio, where he entered grade school.

He prepped at the Marion Military Institute in Marion, Alabama, entering the Naval Academy in 1923. He graduated from the Academy in 1927.

As an Ensign on the battleship, California, he married Grace Fulwood of Tifton, Georgia.
He served in the destroyers, Buchanan, Philip, Aaron Ward, the supply ship Arctic and heavy cruiser Augusta, the destroyer Cummings, and the Ward. Subsequent commands included the O'Brien, Destroyer Division 42, Destroyer Squadron 4, and the heavy cruiser Los Angeles.
He retired in 1957, at which time he was promoted to the rank of Rear Admiral.

INSTRUMENT OF SURRENDER

We, acting by command of and in behalf of the Emperor of Japan, the Japanese Government and the Japanese Imperial General Headquarters, hereby accept the provisions set forth in the declaration issued by the heads of the Governments of the United States, China and Great Britain on 26 July 1945, of Potsdam, and subsequently adhered to by the Union of Soviet Socialist Republics, which four powers are hereafter referred to as the Allied Powers.

We hereby proclaim the unconditional surrender to the Allied Powers of the Japanese Imperial General Headquarters and of all Japanese armed forces and all armed forces under Japanese control wherever situated.

We hereby command all Japanese forces wherever situated and the Japanese people to cease hostilities forthwith, to preserve and save from damage all ships, aircraft, and military and civil property and to comply with all requirements which may be imposed by the Supreme Commander for the Allied Powers or by agencies of the Japanese Government of his direction.

We hereby command the Japanese Imperial General Headquarters to issue at once orders to the Commanders of all Japanese forces and all forces under Japanese control wherever situated to surrender unconditionally themselves and all forces under their control.

We hereby command all civil, military and naval officials to obey and enforce all proclamations, orders and directives deemed by the Supreme Commander for the Allied Powers to be proper to effectuate this surrender and issued by him or under his authority and we direct all such officials to remain at their posts and to continue to perform their non-combatant duties unless specifically relieved by him or under his authority.

We hereby undertake for the Emperor, the Japanese Government and their successors to carry out the provisions of the Potsdam Declaration in good faith, and to issue whatever orders and take whatever action may be required by the Supreme Commander for the Allied Powers or by any other designated representative of the Allied Powers for the purpose of giving effect to that Declaration.

We hereby command the Japanese Imperial Government and the Japanese Imperial General Headquarters at once now under Japanese control and to provide for their protection, care, maintenance and immediate transportation to places as directed.

The authority of the Emperor and the Japanese Government to rule the state shall be subject to the Supreme Commander for the Allied Powers who will take such steps as he deems proper to effectively ...

Signed at ___TOKYO BAY, JAPAN___ at ___0904 T___

on the ___SECOND___ day of ___SEPTEMBER___ , 1945

By Command and in behalf of the Emperor of Japan
and the Japanese Government.

By Command and in behalf of the Japanese
Imperial General Headquarters.

Accepted at ___TOKYO BAY, JAPAN___ at ___0908 T___

on the ___SECOND___ day of ___SEPTEMBER___ , 1945

for the United States, Republic of China, United Kingdom and the Union of Soviet Socialist Republics, and in
the interests of the other United Nations at war with Japan.

Supreme Commander for the Allied Powers

United States Representative

Republic of China Representative

United Kingdom Representative

Union of Soviet Socialist Republics
Representative

Commonwealth of Australia Representative

Dominion of Canada Representative

Provisional Government of the French
Republic Representative

Kingdom of the Netherlands Representative

Dominion of New Zealand Representative

RAYMOND PAUL WOODS

To you who answered the call of your country and served in its Armed Forces to bring about the total defeat of the enemy, I extend the heartfelt thanks of a grateful Nation. As one of the Nation's finest, you undertook the most severe task one can be called upon to perform. Because you demonstrated the fortitude, resourcefulness and calm judgment necessary to carry out that task, we now look to you for leadership and example in further exalting our country in peace.

Harry Truman

THE WHITE HOUSE

WWII: Saving the world

The generation now passing deserves our respect.

They're not getting any younger, and there are fewer every day — America's World War II generation.

They may seem like any other group of old people, mostly retirees now, just old men and women on porches, in nursing homes, parents and grandparents — but they're not.

When they were young, they saved the world.

Remarkable how completely ordinary it seems.

No other generation in world history can make that claim.

Not the Founders of the American Revolution, the ancient Greeks and Romans, nor the baby boomers — not even the early Christians.

Other generations had great struggles; other times had great challenges; but at best here and there were saviors of a town or a country, vanguards of unfulfilled promises, dreamers of visions.

By Paul Donnelly, a Hyattsville, Md., writer.

America's World War II generation did not, as a group, achieve the heroism of an individual like Joan of Arc, nor is there any evidence that their "souls were touched by fire," as Oliver Wendell Holmes Jr. described the experience of the Civil War when he had grown old.

But isn't it fitting that victory in the most intense, deadly and important struggle in human history should seem sort of ordinary to those who won it, and those who benefited?

America's World War II generation saved the world because it had to be done, and no one else was available to do it.

It isn't that America's Vietnam generation, for example, both the pro and the con, couldn't or wouldn't have saved the world.

They didn't get the chance.

It isn't that Russians, who actually broke the *Wehrmacht*, or Chinese, who held Japan's best troops in a death grip, or British or French or any of the rest of the world's peoples, didn't win the war.

But they didn't save the world from an unspeakable global evil.

That was the Americans — when, as Winston Churchill said, the "new world came to the rescue of the old."

But they weren't vast forces of history, or legendary warriors. They weren't even all combat soldiers, or Rosie the Riveters.

They were ordinary people — my Uncle Ed, and your mom and dad — who lived in an extraordinary time.

So they did what had to be done.

There was a fair amount of ballyhoo last December, at the 50th anniversary of Pearl Harbor, although it got sticky with tensions in the current U.S.-Japan relationship.

In a few years, there will be lots of half-century anniversaries of V-E and V-J Day, maybe some prayerful ceremonies honoring liberation of the death camps.

The ex-Soviet republics might pause to remember that there was once a place called Stalingrad, and it was very important.

There will be fewer alive then who actually did those things, though.

So what that 50 years ago today, or last week, or next year, a lot of people killed and died for famous victories?

This isn't about anniversaries, or the all-World War II newsreel channel that every cable TV system seems to have. It's about the old guy you see on the street, with a little poppy in his lapel, or the blue-haired woman who forgets things and who rides the bus.

Let's take a long, last look at these people now, while we still have a chance.

No one has ever done anything like their achievement before — and God willing, no one will ever have to do anything like it again.

CHAPTER 13

USS O'BRIEN DD725

RECOMMISSIONED

OCTOBER 5, 1950

SAN DIEGO, CALIFORNIA

RECOMMISSIONING CEREMONY OCTOBER 5, 1950

l to R - Skipper USS Cunningham (DD752), Commodore Ford, Flag Commander USS O'Brien (DD725), Skipper of USS Walke (DD723), and Commander Chester W. Nimitz, JR. USS O'Brien (DD725).

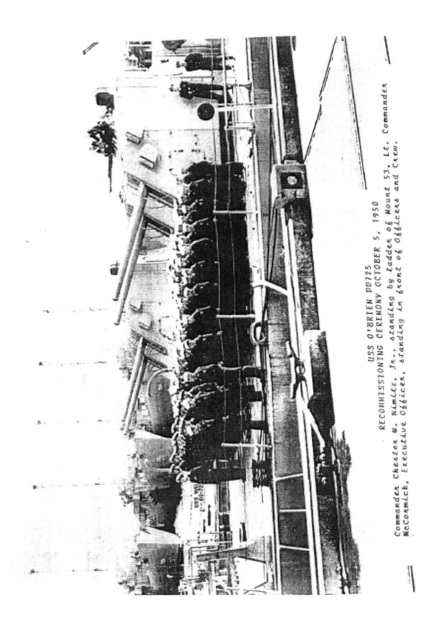

USS O'BRIEN DD725
RECOMMISSIONING CEREMONY OCTOBER 5, 1950

Commander Chester W. Nimitz, Jr., standing by ladder of Mount 53, Lt. Commander McCormick, Executive Officer, standing in front of Officers and Crew.

USS O'BRIEN DD725
RECOMMISSIONING CEREMONY OCTOBER 5, 1950

MIDWAY ISLAND DECEMBER 1, 1956
O'Brien and Hubbard Fueling Dock

O'BRIEN'S CAMPAIGN RIBBONS DISPLAYED ON STBD BRIDGE
AUGUST 1957
(She would earn three (3) more Battle Stars
and suffer six (6) casualties (2 killed and
4 wounded) some ten (10) years later off the
Coast of Vietnam.

Obie's a registered setter—
but he's a liberty hound too.

CDR William Self, captain of O'Brien
works with Obie sitting by his side.

As USS O'Brien heads out to sea, sea dog Obie
and a shipmate say goodbye to Long Beach

Obie descends a ladder with an
Irish potato, a favorite snack

LONG BEACH HARBOR, AUGUST 1957

DICTIONARY OF
AMERICAN NAVAL
FIGHTING SHIPS
VOLUME V – 1970

O'BRIEN operated in the eastern Pacific, Hawaii, the Marianas, and Australia through the first half of 1947. She returned to the west coast in the summer and decommissioned at San Diego, California, 4 October 1947.

Three years later she recommissioned at San Diego, on 5 October 1950, Comdr. C. W. Nimitz, Jr. in command, and became the flagship of Destroyer Division 132.

During the Korean War she first joined the TF 77 carrier group in early March 1951. Later that month she joined TF 95, the United Nations Blockading and Escort Force, and participated in the siege of Songin. On 17 July 1951, at Wonsan Harbor, shore batteries opened on O'BRIEN, BLUE and CUNNINGHAM from three sides in a futile attempt to drive UN vessels from the harbor. The ships went at once into the "War Dance," an evasive maneuver in which ships steamed in an ellipse at 22 knots firing on batteries in each sector as their guns came to bear. This four and a half hour engagement became known as the "Battle of the Buzzsaw."

In July and August O'BRIEN provided covering fire for LSMR bombardment, and coordinated rescue operations which saved three downed Navy pilots and one Air Force pilot. Although both Radio Moscow and Radio Peking reported O'BRIEN sunk by the North Korean Peoples Army, she returned to San Diego for repairs in late September 1951. On 23 July 1952, she returned to Korea as part of TF 95 and participated in shore bombardment, interdiction and patrol duties near Wonsan Harbor. Ordered to the 7th Fleet with HELENA (CA-75), she provided search and rescue protection for carrier aircraft and shore bombardment fire on the east coast of Korea in September. The ship joined Operation "Feing," a mock invasion of Koo 12-16 October 1952, in which UN forces attempted to lure the enemy into the open. At then end of the month, she left the Korean area for exercises and repairs in Japan before returning to San Diego in mid-January 1953.

From the end of the Korean action through 1960, O'BRIEN made annual operational cruises to the western Pacific. In late January and early February 1955, she operated with WASP when the 7th Fleet discouraged Communist resistance to the Nationalist evacuation of the Tachen Islands off the Chinese mainland.

February to October 1961 was spent in Mare Island Naval Shipyard. Vallejo, California for FRAM II conversion. The ship now specialized in antisubmarine Warfare Group I, she was one of the first ships successfully to refuel a helicopter from HORNET off San Francisco while it made a pioneer nonstop helicopter flight from Seattle, Washington to Imperial Beach, California.

The ship sailed for 7th Fleet duty in August and was assigned to Taiwan patrol. On 14 November 1965, while patrolling the Taiwan Straits, the ship was ordered to the aid of a Chinese Nationalist patrol craft under attack by Communist torpedo boats. Arriving after the vessel had sunk, she rescued all fifteen survivors, and was praised by Commander in Chief, National Chinese Navy.

A week later, 22 November 1965, more than 600 miles from the rescue, O'BRIEN saw her first action in the Vietnam War. Called to the aid of a surrounded outpost at Thach Teu, Quang Ngai province, the ship's accurate fire helped turn back a North Vietnamese regiment. In January and early February 1966, she supported carrier operations, conducted search and rescue missions in the Tonkin Gulf and provided gunfire support for the amphibious landing near Cape Batangan, Operation "Double Eagle."

O'BRIEN returned to her homeport March 1966 and operated on the west coast for the next eight months. During a port visit to The Dalles, Oregon, in July O'BRIEN became the largest vessel to use the locks as the Bonneville Dam and to transit the Columbia River to The Dalles.

The destroyer got underway again for the troubled western Pacific, 5 November 1966. Following antisubmarine warfare exercises in Hawaii and the eastern South China Sea, O'BRIEN became flagship for Operation "Sea Dragon," the surface action task unit off North Vietnam. With MADDOX (DD731), she was ordered to interdict enemy coastal traffic. More then twenty vessels carrying enemy war supplies to the Viet Cong were sunk or damaged by O'BRIEN. On 23 December 1966, the ship received three direct hits from coastal batteries north of Dong Hoe. Two crewmen were killed and four wounded. After repairs at Subic Bay, P.I., she provided support for air strikes from Tonkin Gulf while guarding five different carriers in January 1967. In February and March, she was assigned to Taiwan patrol. The ship returned to the Tonkin Gulf in late March, first as a carrier escort and then on "Sea Dragon" operations. Again as flagship for Commander, Destroyer Division 232, she was instrumental in significantly slowing coastal supply traffic. She was taken under fire by shore batteries seven times during this period.

The ship returned to her homeport of Long Beach, California, in May 1967. In July 1967 she made a second trip to The Dalles, Oregon, before entering Long Beach Naval Shipyard for overhaul. Following refresher training at San Diego, she was assigned to the 7th Fleet operations in the spring of 1968.

* * * * *

The USS O'BRIEN (DD725) earned one (1) battle star on the European –
African – Middle Eastern Area Service Ribbon, for participating in the fol-
lowing operation:
1 Star / Invasion of Normandy (including bombardment of Cherbourg) 6-25
June 1944.
The (DD725) also earned five (5) battle stars on the Asiatic – Pacific Area
Service Ribbon, for participating in the following operations:

1   Star / Leyte Operation
         Luzon Attacks -- 15, 17-19 October 1944; 5-6, 13-14, 19-25
         November 1944; and 14-16 December 1944.
         Ormoc Bay Landing -- 7-13 December 1944.

1   Star / Luzon Operation
         Mindoro Landing – 12-18 December 1944.
         Lingayen Gulf Landing – 4-18 January 1945.

1   Star / Iwo Jima Operation
         Assault and Occupation of Iwo Jima – 15 February to 16 March
         1945.
         FIFTH Fleet raids against Konshu and the Nansei Shoto – 15
         February to 16 March 1945.

1   Star / Okinawa Gunton Operation
         Assault and Occupation of Okinawa Gunto – 24 March to 30 June
         1945.

1   Star / Consolidation of the Southern Philippines
         Windanao Island Landings (including Zambonga, Malabang,
         Panang-Sotabato Davao Gulf – Digos – Santa Cruz – Taloma Bay –
         Luayon Cape San Augustin, Macajalar Bay, Sarangani Bay – Balut
         Island) – 8 March to 20 July 1945.

USS O'BRIEN DD725 - BATTLE STARS

(Please note it is stated elsewhere that three battle stars were received for the Vietnam Service – according to later information received, there were eight battle stars for the Vietnam Service.)

KOREAN WAR:

1   Star / First U.N. Counter Offensive: 9 March to 7 April 1951.

1   Star / Communist China Spring Offensive: 13-23 May and 20-27 June 1951.

1   Star / U.N. Summer-Fall Offensive: 11 July to 8 August and 22 August – 21 September 1951.

1   Star / Korean Defense: 23 July to 3 August and 3-27 September and 5-25 October 1952.

1   Star / Third Korean Winter: 10-22 December 1952.

VIETNAM WAR:

1   Star / Vietnam Defense Campaign: 18-24 November 1965.

1   Star / Vietnamese Counter Offensive Campaign: 16 January to 2 February 1966.

1   Star / Vietnamese Counter Offensive Campaign, Phase II: 20-24 December and 31 March to 17 April 1966.

1   Star / Vietnamese Counter Offensive, Phase IV: 24-30 June 1968.

1   Star / Vietnamese Counter Offensive, Phase V: 1-20 July and 28-29 July and 23 August to September and 8-20 October 1968.

1   Star / Vietnam, Winter-Spring 1970: 8 December 1969 to 4 January 1970; 18 February to 8 March and 20-26 March and 4-20 April and 6 May to 5 June and 20-29 June 1970.

1   Star / Vietnamese Counter Offensive, Phase VII: 28 July to 3 August and 15-19 December 1970; 12 January to 1 February and 20 February to 8 April and 3-123 May to 18 June and 29 June to 30 June 1971.

1   Star / Consolidation I: 1-21 July and 1-5 September 1971.

* * * * *

This is the year 2012 and I am eighty-nine years old but I must admit tears came into my eyes seeing the picture of my ship, the USS O'Brien DD725, being taken to its final burial ground at sea in the Pacific. This ship that I was on when it was placed into commission in February 1944 and had kept me safe for two years during six invasions in the Pacific and D-Day Normandy at Omaha Beach and the bombardment of Cherbourg and fought in two more wars earning 6 Battle Stars in Korea and 8 Battle Stars in Vietnam.

All that's left of the O'Brien years later at a Ships Reunion in St. Louis – the helm that I used to help steer the O'Brien back from Okinawa brought back memories.

All I can think of to write now is:

Well Done, Oh Ship of Fate
We shipmates who are still alive, Salute You!

REFERENCES

Newspaper Articles:
    "Costly Battle Due on Luzon", by V.P. Ressel, S. Moore
    "Hero Vessel Under Repair at M.I." (Navy Yard), Times Herald – Vallejo, California, July 13, 1945
    "New US Fleet off Mindoro, Jap Wait Invasion of Luzon"
    "Ships" (Time Magazine, January 7, 1945)
    "US Jabs off Luzon have Japs Punchy", by VP Mec. R. Johnson, January 8, 1944
    "WWII Saving the World", by Paul Donnelly, Hyattsville, MD Winter
    "Yanks Deep Inland on Luzon Astride Highways to Manila", by VP William C. Wilson, January 10, 1944
    "Yanks Strike Deep into Mindoro after 600 Mile Jump from Leyte", by William B. Dickinson, December 16, 1943; December 19, 1943

Radiograms and Ship Log pages are copies of originals.